"I wish you were thirteen again so you'd understand!" I shouted my usual line to my mother before going into my room and slamming the door. My pocketbook, binoculars, bike chain and lock, hanging from the doorknob, clinked and jangled for a full minute afterward, possibly even waking up my father and Jillie. They both sleep like logs, as my grandfather would say—whatever that means.

I reached into my desk drawer for this notebook that I write in, usually when I'm angry. I scribbled a couple of sentences.

MEMO: To myself when I have a teenage kid. It will not have a sister two years younger, and I will never forget what it feels like to be thirteen.

CAROL SNYDER was born and raised in Brooklyn. She is the author of several books for young readers. In addition to writing, she lectures and teaches a writers' workshop.

Memo: To Myself
When I Have A Teenage Kid

CAROL SNYDER

Pacer BOOKS FOR YOUNG ADULTS

B

BERKLEY BOOKS, NEW YORK

This Berkley/Pacer books contains the complete
text of the original hardcover edition.

MEMO: TO MYSELF WHEN I HAVE A TEENAGE KID

A Berkley/Pacer Book, published by arrangement
with Coward-McCann, Inc.

PRINTING HISTORY
Coward-McCann edition / 1983
Berkley/Pacer edition / 1984

ISBN: 0-425-09967-9
RL: 5.0

Pacer is a trademark belonging to
The Putnam Publishing Group.

A BERKLEY BOOK ® TM 757,375
Berkley Books are published by The Berkley Publishing Group,
200 Madison Avenue, New York, NY 10016.
The name "Berkley" and the "B" logo
are trademarks belonging to Berkley Publishing Corporation.

PRINTED IN THE UNITED STATES OF AMERICA

10   9   8   7

MEMO: To Mickey, Amy and Linda—
I love you!

Contents

Never Do Today What You
  Can Put Off Till Tomorrow   11

Complications   21

The Gift   31

Dad at Thirteen   41

Ma and Pa Bell Against Me   48

Answers and More Questions   57

Announcements   65

Everything Snowballs   72

Meanwhile, Back at the Ranch House   80

Double Trouble   92

At the Hospital and Home Again   101

The Fabulous Fifties . . . Yawn   112

Mr. X Marks the Spot   123

The Party   133

The Diary   148

Memo: To Myself

When I Have A Teenage Kid

1

Never Do Today What You
Can Put Off Till Tomorrow

"Beth, let me in! I'll be late for school." I knocked on the bathroom door. "You've been in there twenty minutes already. Did you fall in?"

"Can't a person have any privacy?" Beth called back.

"If a person has a private bathroom then a person can have all the privacy she wants. But you don't happen to have one. Come on, Beth. Let me in. I just want to brush my teeth."

"No. You take an hour to blow-dry your hair and you never let me in."

"I do so," I said, turning the doorknob. No luck. The door was locked.

My sister Beth is eleven, two years younger than I am, and she's discovered the mirror, my makeup, and a million ways to make me crazy.

"Okay Beth—that's it!" I threatened. "You're never wearing my barrettes again."

"Girls!" Mom called from her bedroom. "How can you fight at seven o'clock in the morning? You haven't even been up long enough to have something to fight about."

I think that if Beth and I shared a room, we would fight

in our sleep. I'm lucky to have my own room, at least for six months out of the year. That's when we trade our little sister Jill. Jillie's always been the "baby" to us. Even now when she's in kindergarten. For some reason neither of us fights with her. But since Jillie was born, Beth and I have been fighting more than ever before. Beth has her in her room for these six months, I get her in my room in the spring. Jillie thinks it's neat to have two rooms.

"Beth, if you're not out of the bathroom in the next second, I'm hiding your shoes and you won't find them until you're fifty-three."

Beth flushed the toilet, but she didn't come out. She turned on the faucet and called, "Ha-ha, Karen. I have my shoes on."

I kicked the door.

"Girls! Cut it out this minute!" my mother called.

"I wish you were thirteen again so you'd understand!" I shouted my usual line to my mother before going into my room and slamming the door. My pocketbook, binoculars, bike chain and lock, hanging from the doorknob, clinked and jangled for a full minute afterward, possibly even waking up my father and Jillie. They both sleep like logs, as my grandfather would say—whatever that means.

I reached into my desk drawer for this notebook that I write in, usually when I'm angry. I scribbled a couple of sentences.

MEMO: To myself when I have a teenage kid.
It will not have a sister two years younger, and I will
never forget what it feels like to be thirteen.

"Bruno," I said to my pet parakeet, "you're the only one who listens to me. This is a big day for me and Beth's going to make me late." Bruno cocked his head. He's so little. That's why I gave him a big-sounding name.

I reached for the box of birdseed I keep in my room and poured some into Bruno's dish, then went to the window. The birds around here in New Jersey look too skinny in the winter. How do they find food in all this snow anyway? I opened the window a bit and brushed the snow off the feeder. I poured in some seeds, as I do every morning, only this morning there wouldn't be time for any bird watching. A cold breeze made me shiver and I shut the window. I was about to close my curtain when I saw him. I looked at my clock. Seven o'clock. Right on schedule.

"There's that old man again, Bruno," I said, watching the man with the crooked walking stick. "One of these days I'm going to talk to him and find out who he is, where he walks to every day, and why he stops to look at my house. Maybe tomorrow I'll ask him."

My breath steamed up the frosty pane. Even though I was in a hurry I couldn't resist drawing a heart with my fingertip and initialing it K.B. and P.R. for me, Karen Berman, and for Peter Raskin, the boy I help in math. The boy I love—secretly of course. So secretly even he doesn't know it. Maybe he'd kind of get a hint today. If I finally decide to ask him to the school Winter Switch Dance.

I have successfully ignored making my decision for a week now. Tickets go on sale today and the dance is only three days away. I'm very good at putting things off. My father is too. He said we should join the Procrastinators' Club. There really is such a group. They celebrate the Fourth of July in December.

If only I were more like Allison, my best friend in school. She decided to ask this boy, Jeff, to the Winter Switch Dance. And she did it. Asked him right in Science the very same day the dance was announced. But, then, Allison also packs her suitcase three days before she goes to her grandmother's. And her mother sets the table for breakfast the night before.

Why do they have to have this dumb dance anyway, I wondered, hurriedly getting dressed. Girls asking boys must be Madison School's easy answer to women's lib. But I'm already liberated. Sometimes I'm embarrassed because my liberated family does things differently from my friends' families. I wish I didn't get embarrassed so easily.

I finished dressing and stuffed some of my baby-sitting money into my pocket to pay for the dance tickets. Then I put blue heart earrings in my pierced ears and pulled on new striped socks. I'd been saving these socks for a special occasion, and without a doubt, today would be it. New socks gave me confidence. I felt better already—until I couldn't find my blue barrettes.

I walked to the still shut bathroom door, knocked, and shouted, "Beth! You and my blue barrettes better get out here this minute."

She opened the door. "I was coming out anyway," she said, and sauntered to her room.

Somehow she always gets the last word. My barrettes were just sitting there by the sink. I brushed my teeth and used the Water Pik till my braces glistened.

The split separating the mirrored medicine-chest doors divided my face in half. That's just how I felt too. Part of me wants to decide things for myself and do them, and part of me won't even make my own orthodontist appointment. I brushed my hair until it was real shiny brown. My hair is long, so I shampooed it three times last night to make sure it wouldn't be greasy. Now I struggled to get my barrettes in straight, then dashed down the hall to the kitchen.

I was at the counter fixing my own breakfast when Mom appeared. She was wearing her really soft yellow robe. I can't wait till I grow into it.

"Morning," Mom said. "Are you the sole survivor of the morning battle?" She flipped the window shade up and the glare blinded me. She kissed me, missing my cheek and landing on my forehead. I gave her a quick kiss back. She looked half asleep and feeling her way around. She must've been up almost all night, writing. She says lots of writers do that.

"It's snowing hard, Karen, you'd better wear boots."

I took a container of milk from the refrigerator, which is covered with magnets holding school notices, Jillie's drawings, flyers about concerts and lectures, and recommended restaurants in New York.

"It snowed last night," she repeated, "and it's still snowing. So wear boots."

"*Boots,*" I whined. "No one wears boots to school. They'll laugh me right out of class if I wear *boots*! I won't do it!"

"That's ridiculous," Mom said as she filled the coffee maker with water. "If there's snow on the ground you wear boots. It's supposed to get worse—four to six inches the radio said."

"I'm not two years old, you know," I answered, pouring the milk into my bowl so fast that it overflowed, sending a white river flowing down the counter with cornflakes floating like dead leaves. I mopped it up with the sponge.

"Do what you want," Mom said. "But if you go out without boots, it's your decision. And I don't want to hear any complaints later about ruined shoes or cold feet." She plugged in the coffee maker and headed back to her room without stopping. Her slippers made a flapping noise that you could hear even when you could no longer see her. I wish my mother would stop treating me like a baby. Since I'd lost my appetite, I rinsed my dish and put it in the dishwasher.

I grabbed my jacket from the hall closet and was about to take my bootless feet out the door when my father appeared in his terry-cloth robe. Having your father work at home is like having two mothers, I thought. He's an inventor, and his laboratory is down in our basement.

"You look beautiful," Dad said to me. "Nice outfit."

"Thanks," I said, throwing him a kiss. I like when my father notices how I look or says he's proud of me for my good math paper.

"Zip up your jacket—and you'd better wear boots, Karen," Dad said. The whirr of the juicer didn't drown out my loud answer.

"If I hear one more person say boots I'LL SCREAM!"

"Boots! Boots! Boots, boots, boots!" Jillie came into the kitchen and danced around.

"I am not putting on boots! I wish you were thirteen again so you'd understand," I screamed at my dad, and headed for the door.

How could I wear brown fuzz-lined boots on the day I was asking Peter to the dance? No one would want to go to a dance with Bigfoot!

Dad cracked an egg, hitting it harder than usual against the counter edge, then setting it sizzling in the frying pan.

I remembered the baby robin I once watched crack its way out of a beautiful pale blue eggshell. I remembered wishing it would just nibble its way out of a corner and keep the shell to climb back into now and then. I saved the shell. It's on my dresser someplace.

"I'm leaving," I called behind me as I closed the back door.

The snow slipped into the sides of my shoes, and my new striped socks felt as soggy as my confidence. I clutched my books and looked down the block. The old man who stares at my house every day was out of sight by now, but I could see his footprints in the snow along with the mark from his walking stick.

I looked up ahead to the bus stop. Peter was there. He's the kind of kid who stands out in a crowd. Not because he's so tall but because he's so lively. He had a snowball in his hand. I hoped I was going to be the target.

I was not about to ask Peter Raskin to the dance while we waited together at the bus stop. The cold wind was making my nose run, and how can you ask a boy to a dance when you're busy with a tissue? Maybe I wasn't going to ask him at all. Maybe he only pays attention to me because he wants me to keep on helping him in math. He didn't seem to notice me as I came up to the bus stop.

Peter was laughing and swinging around on a loose stop sign. His shirt was half untucked and hanging out of his jacket, as usual. It just makes him look active, not sloppy. I love his laugh. It sounds so real and happy, not forced or weird like some kids' laughs. Today he even waved to me and called hello. My heart raced as I waved back.

I was about to go right up to him and ask him to the dance when he called, "Did you get 658 or 568 meters as your answer for Problem D?"

"Let me see your paper and I'll check it with mine," I said. Peter usually knows the right answer, but he sometimes writes it down wrong.

Then I saw that this other girl, Dana, was holding Peter's books. Peter glanced from her to me and added, "Thanks, Karen. I'll show you my paper before class."

And then, worst of all, Peter threw a snowball—not at me but at Dana, and I really got worried.

I've learned a lot about boys because my very best friend is a boy named Scott. He told me the truth about snowballs. Scott said if a boy throws a snowball at you it means he likes you in a boyfriend/girlfriend way. Unless it's in self-defense, of course. But when a boy dumps snow on your head or pushes it in your face, it just means friendship. And it was Dana who was spotted white with the remains of Peter's carefully aimed snowballs.

For all I knew, maybe Dana had already asked Peter to the dance. She wasn't the shy type. She even smoked cigarettes and called them grits to act really cool. Dana cursed a lot too, especially around teachers.

By the time Scott arrived I was too depressed to even scoop up a handful of snow and push it in his face.

I looked at Scott. We're the same size, so we can look right into each other's eyes. His skin was red from the cold and his blond hair was frosted with snowflakes. One thing I like about Scott is that you don't have to tell him your feelings. He just knows.

We didn't have time to talk. The bus skidded to a halt in front of me and the doors made that familiar squeal as they opened. I was propelled onto the bus by the herd of bootless kids behind me, shoving in spite of the bus driver's pleas of "Don't push!" and "Settle down, kids!" Scott sat down across the aisle. We don't share a seat on the bus, but it's okay to talk to each other. Lots of kids lean into the aisle and whisper, but a girl sharing a seat with a boy, every day, means more than just friendship. We don't even talk much in school. For some reason, in school we're shy about being best friends.

"Don't tell a soul," Scott said, leaning across the aisle and whispering, "especially not your mother, because she'll tell my mother and they'll say 'How cute,' but Lori Blake called me up last night. She asked me to the Winter Switch Dance. It's a good thing I answered the phone, not my mother."

"What did you tell Lori?" I asked.

"I told her I'd think it over and let her know today."

"What did you do that for?" Forgetting for a minute that we were in public, I reached across the narrow aisle and gently punched Scott in the shoulder. "Why didn't you just say yes? She's a real nice kid."

"I didn't know what to say," Scott said. "I'll tell her in school."

Just then the bus skidded slightly on the snow-covered road and we had to grab onto our books and our seats as best we could. Dana's books went flying, probably on purpose.

"Hey, Peter!" she yelled. "Help me pick up my damn books."

For the rest of the trip I couldn't stop staring at Peter helping Dana.

The bus stopped and doors screeched open. When I got out I looked up the block and saw that old man again. Still walking. Right on schedule. Kids leaped or stepped out of the bus and raced up the path to the big wide doors of Madison School. Scott and I waved. We wouldn't see each other again until later.

It was still snowing pretty hard I noticed as I waved to Allison. We walked together down the path. I didn't dare look back. Peter and Dana giggled behind me. Then I saw Dana dash off across the path to the side door. Just as I got to the front entrance a snowball smacked my back.

"See you in math," Peter called to me and raced ahead, looking like an Olympic track star finalist.

Allison bumped my shoulder with hers and we giggled.

"Maybe Peter does like me," I whispered. "Maybe Dana didn't ask him yet. Maybe I'll ask him to the dance during math."

"But the tickets will be on sale before that," Allison reminded me, "and they sell out fast."

"What if I buy two tickets and he says no? I don't have money to throw away like that," I said, catching a pad that was slipping from Allison's mountain of books.

"But what if you don't buy tickets and he would have said yes?" She raised her eyebrows to emphasize the problem. She never seems to have trouble making decisions by herself. I always seem to need a vote. I ask my mom, my dad, Beth, Scott, Allison. Sometimes I even ask Jillie and my pet parakeet, Bruno.

I walked inside the school, adding my muddy footsteps to the trail already there on the shiny waxed floor. Scott had a date, Allison had a date, and all I had was a problem.

2

Complications

I struggled with my miserable lock, then stuffed my jacket and junk into my locker. Jangling, slamming locker sounds made my eardrums pound. Voices giggled, buzzed, and shouted. But in almost every conversation I heard that word "tickets."

"C'mon." Allison tugged at my blouse. "We better get to homeroom and get ready for the ticket sale." I felt as if I had roller skates on as Allison propelled me down the hall and into Room 207.

I kind of collapsed into my seat and half listened as the static on the intercom got my attention and announcements were made. My heart beat faster when the monotonous voice said, "Tickets for the seventh grade Sadie Hawkins Day Winter Switch Dance will go on sale in the library following these announcements. You will have ten minutes to purchase your tickets in an orderly way on a first-come-first-served basis. Because of the small size of Madison School's all-purpose room where the dance will be held, only a limited number of tickets will be sold."

No one listened to the rest of the announcements. Even faster than for a fire drill, the girls raced toward the doorway.

Now what? I said to myself, feeling as if my wet socks and shoes had turned to Krazy Glue and I was permanently stuck to this spot. I had to make up my mind about buying tickets.

I caught up with the rest of the seventh grade girls stampeding through the hallway to the library. I felt myself bumped and jostled and almost lost one of my quarters when it dropped and I had to bend down and find it. Maybe it was an omen—it must mean that I shouldn't buy tickets. That Peter will say no.

I made a quick bet with myself; heads I buy tickets, tails I don't. I guess I really wanted to go to the dance, because I hoped for heads and was glad to see the familiar but slightly worn-out thin face of George Washington as I picked up my quarter.

"C'mon"—Allison waved to me from her spot, closer to the front of the line—"I'll give you fronts."

I started to step into the space she made, but the girl behind Allison called, "Get out of here. You cut." And Mr. Bush, the assistant principal, was nearby.

"Thanks anyway," I said.

Allison just shrugged her shoulders.

With Mr. Bush staring at me, I didn't even think to give her money to buy my tickets. I walked back to the end of the line. I passed Lori and wondered if Scott had told her yes or no yet. I passed Dana. She was giggling and pushing the girl in front of her. The line weaved all the way down the hall and around the corner to the lockers.

As people got into trouble in line for fighting or whatever, they were sent back, so I wasn't last for very long. Mr. Bush escorted Dana and her friend to the spot right behind me. "Quit pushing me," Dana mumbled. As Mr. Bush walked away, she muttered under her breath, "Damn you." She even cursed at the assistant principal. She was lucky he didn't hear her.

"Who you gonna go with?" this tough girl, Gwen Edwards, asked Dana.

I listened, waiting to hear if Dana had asked anyone yet.

But instead of answering out loud, Dana whispered something to Gwen.

I was peeking around the sides to see how far we'd moved when Dana poked me in the shoulder blades to get my attention. I whirled around, so nervous that a little poke felt like a dagger.

"Hey, Karen, you gotta save my life. I'm dying for a grit. Here's my money and Gwen's—buy our damn tickets for us, huh? We'll be in the eighth-wing john. Okay?"

Dana was shoving the money at me and I was working up courage to say "Sorry, find someone else" when she changed her mind.

"Never mind, twirp," she said to me as if I were going to buy the tickets for her. "They'll probably be sold out before you get to the front of the line. Only two hundred measly tickets are on sale, because the all-purpose room is so damn small."

I watched Dana and Gwen race ahead and push their money into this other girl's accepting palm. Dana either talks as if she's mad at the world or clowns around until she's in trouble.

The line of kids moved up a bit, then stopped. I started daydreaming. Daydreams are so nice. Everyone does just what you want them to do, and if you say a wrong thing in a daydream you can kind of erase it and do it over. In my mind I asked Peter to the dance and of course he said yes, he'd hoped I'd ask him. The line was moving faster now. I was almost next. I couldn't believe it when the girl selling tickets closed the metal cash box right in front of my nose and announced, "Sorry, sold out!"

I could hardly hear her explanation as the kids on the line pleaded for tickets. "Fire laws don't allow more than two hundred kids in the all-purpose room at the same time. It's not my fault," the girl said.

"Sold out?" My voice sounded like a siren signaling an emergency. "You can't do this to me, you just can't."

I walked to my Social Studies class, where I hardly paid attention to Mrs. Horagian. Besides being boring, she's the kind of teacher who only seems to smile when she gives back tests that kids have failed. Actually no one paid attention. Most of the kids were all busy watching the snow fall.

In the background I could hear the buzzing of kids taking bets on whether we'd only have a half day of school, but I didn't pay much attention until Bruce Mason said, "It's sure snowing hard now. Maybe we'll be sent home right after lunch."

"Yeah," I mumbled, not really listening. I was too disappointed about not getting tickets and too busy worrying. I just had to get tickets and ask Peter to the dance. There was one possibility left—not exactly an honest way, but if I could work up enough nerve to do it, I'd have the tickets by lunchtime. And maybe Dana had been too busy smoking to ask Peter to the dance.

In my next period English class I looked around for Dana. She wasn't in class yet. Late as usual. Then there was a crash as she came in and slammed the door behind her.

"Oops!" she shrieked, dropping her biggest book. Then she let her pencils roll down the aisle. The kids laughed as she chased her pencils. She let her other books drop. "Damn books!" she cursed.

I stared at my English teacher, who totally ignored Dana's disruption. He's the kind of teacher who tries to be with it but is always at least a year behind. He still says "Right on," or in cases like this, nothing at all. My mind wandered to Peter again.

I was startled when the intercom boomed that low gravelly voice. The secretary cleared her throat, but her voice sounded the same. Kids wiggled in their seats and crossed their fingers, hoping to hear some magic words like "snowday."

"Due to inclement weather," the voice crackled, "this will be the culminating period of your school day."

If she hadn't said the next familiar line, I don't think half the class would have known what she was talking about.

"Throwing snowballs is strictly forbidden!"

"Snowday!" this kid, Brenda, shouted. She was gazing out the window and sharpening her pencil. Everyone cheered and whistled and hooted but me. And I usually love snowdays. But I needed that lunch period in school to find my one chance for tickets. I had to find Joey Dillon, this kid who hires girls to buy tickets for him and then sells the extra tickets at a profit to people who are desperate, like me.

I stared at Dana. She crumpled up the paper in her hands and tossed it as if it were a snowball. She threw it right at the teacher, then got up and ran out of the room, not listening to the teacher calling her back. A wave of kids dashed to the windows to update their bets on how many inches of snow had fallen. Then, with the teacher's words, "Your writing assignment—a letter evoking emotion—is due tomorrow. Class dismissed," ringing in our ears, we headed for our lockers, bundled up, and raced for the frosty air, ready to leave our footsteps in the perfectly smooth snow.

It was when I saw the waiting buses that it really hit me. This dismissal was a definite disaster. Not only couldn't I buy the tickets from Joey at lunch but now I couldn't even catch up with him. He was on bus No. 1, which was just pulling away from the curb as I raced down the path.

Scott caught up with me when his friends were out of sight and we walked to our waiting bus. At first I couldn't get a word in.

"I was going to tell Lori yes at lunch," Scott said. "I haven't seen her yet. Maybe she didn't even buy tickets to the dance."

Scott seemed to wish that were true. I wondered if Peter would feel the same way. "Forget it," I said. "I saw Lori buy tickets. The big problem is *I* didn't get tickets. Wait up a minute." I stopped, bent down and scooped snow out of my shoe. Snowflakes on my eyelashes blurred my sight and I brushed them away.

"You didn't buy them?" Scott asked.

"Sold out right in front of me," I said and sighed my disappointment. "I was going to buy tickets from Joey Dillon at lunch and now there's no lunch period and his bus just pulled away. Do you think I should ask Peter anyway and count on buying the tickets tomorrow?"

"Sure. Absolutely. Ask Peter on the bus," Scott said. "Don't waste any more time."

I felt better now that I had someone else's opinion and encouragement. Why couldn't I make a decision on my own?

Then came the next shock. There was my mother honking the car horn. You can't miss our car. It's a VW bus, with a "No Nukes" bumper sticker. Not only do all the other parents drive normal cars but if they have a sticker at all, it's one that says, "Support Soccer."

"Come on, kids, hop in!" Mom called to us out the rolled-down window. She sounded impatient.

"Hi, Mom," I said.

"Hi, Mrs. Berman," Scott greeted my mother.

He opened the sliding door on the side of the van and gave me a push to help me up the big step. He climbed in and pulled the door shut with a bang.

Mom gave her usual greeting: "You have a good day, kids? Buckle your seat belts," she directed before our bottoms hit the seat. "Daddy and I were notified by the school secretary. As class mothers, we had to notify the other parents that school was canceled. I'd finally gotten to work writing my article—after a morning of baking brownies for Jillie's afternoon kindergarten class—when the phone call came. We've got a lot of brownies at home. I made extras."

"Thanks, Mom." I'm halfway through the year and I don't think I'll ever get used to the fact that I'm the only kid in school whose father is a class mother. Mom was Beth's class mother last year and this year she's Jillie's and Dad's mine.

"Did you pick Beth up at her school too?" I asked.

"No. She went home with a friend," Mom explained. "I arranged it with her friend Cheryl's mother. But since my work was interrupted already, I thought I'd give you guys a lift home today. All this snow—four inches at least." (And no boots, was what Mom really meant.)

As we pulled away I waved to Peter, as if he could see me through the car window. I watched as he and Dana climbed onto the bus. Allison waved from her bus window as we drove past.

We rode down the street, a perfect large green target for the walkers who were armed with "strictly forbidden" snowballs. They thunked against the side of the van. But I felt like those snowballs were hitting me in the stomach as I worried that I wouldn't have the nerve to phone Peter this afternoon. That was the only choice left.

A block later I saw that old man again, walking in all this snow. He wore a green wool cap pulled over his white hair and he used his crooked wooden walking stick to keep his balance. I wished I knew why he walked the same blocks every day as if on a schedule. And why every morning he stops and looks at my house. I definitely planned to be outside the following day when he walked by. And I'd talk to him—if I could think of something to say.

We dropped Scott off and I moved up front next to my mom.

"That Scott is so cute," Mom said. He would have had red cheeks if he heard her.

"MAA-A-A," I sang in what she calls my teenage voice.

Then, glancing at my feet, Mom added, "You are really soaked."

We skidded on some ice as she pulled to a stop in our driveway. Once inside the house we leaned on each other in the hallway as Mom pulled off her boots and I kicked off my soggy shoes.

The warm inside air of home felt good on my chapped cheeks and it smelled good too. The chocolate smell of the brownies made my mouth water. I dumped my books down on the kitchen table. The salt and pepper shakers clunked together.

"Hello up there," Dad called from the basement lab he calls his dungeon.

"Hello down there." I shouted back my usual greeting.

"Hello up there too," Jillie's squeaky voice echoed. "I can't come up. I'm hooked up to Daddy's speriment."

My father's experiments sometimes require a helping

hand—really. In our house, when my dad calls "Could you lend me a hand?" he means your hand. It's hard for me to describe to my friends this work he does—building a bionic hand for the government. They think it's like Frankenstein or something. The hand's almost finished. He's worked on it for three years.

"Karen," Dad called, "if you have a couple of minutes later on, I could use your assistance."

"Sure!" I answered. I love to work with my dad, and I ask him lots of questions. He always answers every one. Sometimes I think he's answering a lot more questions than I'm asking.

But first I followed my mother's beckoning finger. When both of your parents work at home they usually both want you to do something at the same time. Sometimes I feel like a wishbone.

"When's Beth coming home?" I asked.

"Dad'll pick Beth up at Cheryl's just before dinner time," Mom answered. "I've got something for you and I'd like to give it to you alone—just you and me."

"Sure," I said. "Let's go into my room." I was really curious.

"Don't forget your books"—Mom gave me the usual reminder—"the kitchen table is not a dumping ground."

I picked up my books and read a note Beth had left on the table in the morning.

> Dear Karen,
>   Allison called after you left
> and she told me about Peter and
> the dance. Hope Peter said yes.
>   Love,
>   Beth

Beth can be so nice sometimes—in writing anyway. When we were much younger, before Jillie was born, we used to tell each other everything and go everywhere together. Sometimes I miss those days. I don't tell her much anymore.

I followed Mom through the family room and down the hall to my bedroom. I was also relieved to have a good excuse not to phone Peter right away. A few minutes couldn't matter.

3

The Gift

I kicked aside my pajamas and a pair of sneakers as I led Mom into my room. "Hello, Bruno. You been a good bird?" My parakeet fluttered from perch to perch, sending feathers flying. He always does that to greet me. I dumped my books on the already crowded desk and flung my jacket onto the chair, wondering what it was Mom wanted to give me—alone.

"Get comfortable," she said. "I'll be right back."

I propped up my pillows and sat down on the bed. In just a minute Mom returned and sat down next to me between my giant stuffed panda and my stuffed dog. She curled her legs under her and handed me a small tattered box that had a flowery smell and a yellow stain in one corner. The box wasn't big enough for a new pair of jeans and it was too big to be earrings, I thought. I opened it slowly.

Inside was a red-leather diary. I flipped through page after page filled with purple-ink words. The diary was already full. There wasn't a single blank page.

"A used diary?" I asked, looking up.

I saw my mother smile the kind of smile that makes the corners of her eyes wrinkle. She reached for the diary and held it close to her as if it were a friend.

"We used to use fountain pens filled with colored ink." Mom seemed to be talking more to herself than to me. "And the holes you see now and then are from too much ink eradicator, used to bleach out boys' names."

Boyfriends? It was hard to imagine Mom with anyone but my father.

"You're always saying you wish I were thirteen again, so I would understand how you feel," Mom fingered the red leather as she spoke. "I thought about your wish a lot today. I've never showed this diary to another soul. But I'd like to share it with you." Then for the first time that I can remember, I saw my mother blush. "Giving you this diary is my way of giving you myself—your mother at thirteen," she said.

Sometimes I can hold back so many tears that I think I'll drown from the inside out. That's why I was surprised at the tear that trickled down my cheek as Mom handed the diary back to me. I was kind of glad we were alone in my room. I hugged her, leaving a wet spot on the shoulder of her plaid flannel blouse.

Mom hugged me back and reached for the tissues. We blew our noses, sounding like the Madison School band tuning up to play at a dance. We didn't talk. It would have spoiled the moment. I opened the diary to the first page and started reading.

January 1, 1955
Happy New Year, or rather unhappy New Year. In case my rotten sister Judy reads this, I'm not using names. I'll just call him Mr. X—the one I love. If only he were younger. If he would only notice me. My New Year's resolution is to make Mr. X notice me this year.

Mom saw the page I was reading and her cheeks turned even redder.

Then, just at a time when I wanted to be alone, just Mom and me, to ask her about Mr. X, the phone in my room rang.

I knew it must be Allison. I think she has my footsteps timed. She always calls after school just as I get to my room. And she always says "What's new?" What could be new in fifteen minutes? I picked up the phone.

"Hi, Karen, what's new?"

"Hi," I said, and before I could even ask Allison to call back, Mom put the diary on my desk.

"Call me when you're off the phone," she whispered, and walked out of my room, closing the door behind her.

"Listen, Alli, I'll call you later, okay? I've got something important to do now," I explained.

"Good! You're gonna call Peter. Don't give Dana a chance to ask him first, Karen. You can always get tickets from Joey Dillon. Don't let that stop you from asking him. For your own good, you can't wait any longer. Call me back as soon as you ask him."

"Sure. I will," I mumbled. "Bye." I hung up the phone and reached for the leather diary on my desk, convincing myself that I'd be better off waiting a few minutes to call Peter. Sometimes in math, he tells me about his sheep dog. He probably has to walk it when he comes home from school. And I just had to find out more about Mr. X. I curled up in my green beanbag chair and wiggled it into the right shape as if it were a nest.

I flipped through the diary, reading a sentence here and there, looking for more about Mr. X. I didn't know which page to read first. And even more mysterious, it looked like a couple of pages had been ripped out. Were they about

Mr. X? And were they so secret Mom had ripped them out?

For some reason it was hard to think of my mom having secrets. Sure, I had some secrets myself, but they were silly, baby kinds of things. Like once when I was ten and Mom was busy with Beth, I took some change I found in my dad's coat pocket. I spent it on ice cream. Getting ice cream from the ice cream man seemed so important then. I never told anyone about what I'd done. I also didn't enjoy that ice cream pop.

I continued looking through the diary. I found February 2, 1955, and read it. Although it wasn't about Mr. X, it was definitely of interest to me.

> February 2, 1955
> *My mother made me wear a stocking hat today. She even wrapped the long scarf part around my neck. She said I should look at my friend Marsha. "Marsha's wearing one. Her head and neck are covered so she won't get a chill and get pneumonia." And only yesterday when I asked if I could curl my eyelashes like Marsha does, my mother said, "Don't tell me what everyone else is doing." Mothers are nuts! I wore the hat till I got to the corner. Then I unwound it, took it off, and put it behind the bushes. I picked it up on the way home.*

I closed the diary but held it in my lap. "Mom!" I called. "I'm off the phone. Come in."

The door squeaked open and Mom came in. She pushed her long dark hair away from her eyes, then closed the door behind her. I smiled up at her. "You gotta see what I just found in your diary."

Mom pushed aside a pile of dungarees, inside-out socks, and assorted stuffed animals. "Would you like me to draw you a map to the hamper? Or are you waiting for your laundry to walk there by itself?" She sat down next to me on my yellow shag rug. She reached for the open diary that was in my hands. I figured I'd warm her up on the small stuff and then ask about Mr. X and the ripped-out pages.

"Read this," I said. "Sound familiar?"

She read the entry for February 2 and laughed. "Oh yeah, the stocking-hat rebellion," Mom said. "But I did wear boots," and she rumpled my hair.

The phone rang again.

"Don't go," I said to Mom. I wanted to talk about Peter and ask her about Mr. X. Had she ever asked him out? I picked up the phone and heard Allison's voice. "I didn't call him yet," I said. "I'll call you back real soon, Alli. I can't talk now. Bye." I hung up.

"It's scary to ask a boy to this switch dance," I explained to Mom, reaching over and twisting two strands of carpet. "I'd rather have it the old way and let the boys do the asking. I'm afraid of being embarrassed."

Mom was quiet for a minute. Then she said, "You've never done it before, that's why it's scary—like riding a two-wheeler for the first time. I still find things scary too," Mom admitted.

"What?" I asked.

"Driving a car in traffic in New York City, for instance."

For a minute, when my mom talked about her fear and not about my dirty laundry, I felt like we were friends.

"You're a good driver, Mom. I bet you could drive anywhere. Just practice blowing your horn and cursing a lot, like Daddy."

Mom laughed. "Thanks for the vote of confidence," she

said. "One of these days I'll do it."

Mom started flipping through the pages of the diary. Maybe I wouldn't have to ask. Maybe she'd just tell me about Mr. X. For some reason I felt funny asking about something so private that she'd ripped out the pages. Only instead of telling, she started asking. "Do I know the boy you want to go to the dance with?"

"You may have seen him in school the day I was sneezing so much and you had to bring me allergy medicine," I said. "His name is Peter Raskin. He's really nice."

"Raskin," Mom said. "I think I might know his mother from the Parents' Association. I can't say I remember him, though. But if you say he's nice, I'm sure he is."

I stood up to stretch, and glanced at my clock. Three-fifteen. My room is in the front of the house, facing the street. I looked out the window and blinked from the glare of the snow-covered ground. Right on schedule. The old man was walking down the block again. This time I noticed some more about him. He was carrying a transistor radio along with his walking stick, and he wore a green scarf that matched his knitted hat. He looked bundled up. He even wore boots.

"I reread this diary from cover to cover today." Mom got my attention back. "I think, according to my diary, asking a boy to a party is not necessarily a new way. At least it *was* done in Brooklyn in 1955."

I was listening so hard that I'd twisted a piece of yellow carpet till it was loose in my hands. For some reason it became very important to shred it and carefully examine each thread.

Mom turned another page in the diary and stopped. "It's ages ago," she said, "but I can close my eyes and be right there in seventh grade. Schools in Brooklyn don't look like

motels, the way your school does. We had to walk up five
flights of stairs, and the basement smelled like damp
sneakers."

"That hasn't changed," I said, laughing. "Maybe someone invented a new air freshener called 'School Smell.' Our
all-purpose room smells like that. Now tell me about asking
a boy to a party—I want to hear the good stuff." What I
really meant was "Tell me about Mr. X." So why didn't I
just say that? For some reason I couldn't.

Mom laughed and handed me the diary, and I read out
loud the words on that open page.

"Today was very embarrassing," the first line said. I'd
never imagined my mom having an embarrassing moment.
She always seems to say the right thing in public. Feeling
embarrassed makes me wish the floor would swallow me
up. Like last week when I called my teacher "Ma."

I started reading that diary page over.

March 3, 1955
*Today was very embarrassing. I asked Kenny Ross to
go to a party with me. He accepted. As I walked away
I tripped. Then, worst of all was that after asking
him, two girls told me the party was off. So I had to
unask him.*

"At least I don't have to worry about unasking," I said,
kind of leaning against my mom. "This is a definite school
dance." What I have to worry about is asking Peter and
getting tickets from Joey Dillon. Maybe I just wouldn't go,
I thought to myself.

"That boy, Kenny? Did you like him a lot?" I asked. Was
he Mr. X, I was about to add when Mom spoke.

"Actually, I don't think I liked Kenny that much at all,"

she said and laughed. My parakeet, Bruno, fluttered around in the cage, distracting us for a minute. "But I thought Kenny liked me and would say yes," Mom continued. "At the time, I was sure I was in love with someone else, someone who didn't know I was alive. He was older than I was."

"Mr. X?" I finally said.

"Yes," she said and blushed again.

For some reason, finding out Mom liked an older guy who didn't know she was alive made me feel comfortable, because sometimes I think Peter doesn't know I'm alive. All I had to do was think of phoning Peter and I felt uncomfortable again. But somehow I couldn't ask about the ripped-out pages—not yet. Not with Mom blushing when I just said "Mr. X." I also hoped Mom had written a lot about Mr. X in the diary and hadn't ripped it out.

I wondered if I'd remember all the details of my own experiences. Someday if I have a daughter I might want to tell her about them. I liked the way this felt. I decided to write in my notebook of memos to myself if I have a teenage kid: Keep diary. Show it to kid at age thirteen.

Mom got up from the floor and wiggled her foot. "My foot fell asleep," she said, rubbing it.

The phone rang. Allison again. That girl has no patience.

"Not yet. I'm going to call Peter now. How can I call him if I'm on the phone with you all the time? Bye."

I was sorry as soon as I had spoken that way to Allison. I just had to call Peter. Even I know when time is running out.

"I better make that call now," I hinted, to get Mom out of my room. "Maybe we could talk some more later."

"If you want to lock the diary, the key's in the back,"

Mom said, reaching to open the diary that rested in my lap. From the tiny envelope pasted on the inside of the back cover she took out the key. "I always wore it on a chain around my neck," she added, "so your Aunt Judy couldn't get it."

Didn't she know you could open a diary with a bobby pin?

Mom got up and picked a piece of lint off her jeans. She handed the diary back to me, then crossed her fingers to wish me luck.

"You'll know what to say. You'll see," Mom said, walking through the doorway. Then she leaned back in and added, "And you'll know what to do."

I might know what to do, now that we'd talked. Would I ever know what to do if I couldn't talk things over first with Mom, Dad, Scott, or Allison? Would I ever make decisions on my own?

I patted the diary as I walked across my room. I always think better with music blaring, so I pushed the "on" button and turned up the volume of my stereo. My nose itched from the vibration of the loud rock music.

"Karen, you better turn down the stereo," Mom called. "I have to concentrate and type up my article." Obviously my mother was thirty-eight again.

Then I heard the banging. It was Dad banging a broomstick on the basement ceiling. He works right below my room. I got the message and turned off my stereo. With the music off I could hear Dad's equipment beeping from downstairs. And the clicking of Mom's typewriter drove me crazy. I wondered what would happen if I told them to be quiet.

I sat down once more in my beanbag chair.

I couldn't part with the diary yet—I wanted to find out more about my mom at thirteen. Did she ever fight with my Aunt Judy like I fight with Beth? Did she ever get Mr. X to notice her? But I was also hungry. My stomach growled, and I stood up, tucked the diary under my arm, and headed for the kitchen to find the brownies and to look up Peter's number in the phone book.

I took a brownie, picked up crumbs on the tip of my finger, and licked them off. I got the milk from the refrigerator. Then, taking as long as I possibly could, stalling so I wouldn't have to make the phone call, I poured the cold milk into a paper cup and took a gulp of milk and a bite of brownie.

Finally I reached over to the desk for the phone book, creating an avalanche of coupons, newspaper clippings, and scraps of paper covered with notes which had been resting on top of the directory. I piled the papers on the counter top, then took another bite of brownie to fortify myself. I couldn't manage carrying the milk, brownie, and phone book back to my room, so I thumbed through the phone book right in the kitchen.

As if things weren't complicated enough, I couldn't find Peter's number. As hard as I looked, I couldn't find any Raskins in Hillsboro. There were two Raskins in Somerville and one in Greenbrook. Now what? I couldn't wait any longer to ask Peter to the dance! But according to Bell Tel, Hillsboro was Raskinless.

4

Dad at Thirteen

I put the phone book back on Mom's kitchen desk, next to the decorated soup-can pencil holder, a Mother's Day present I'd given her when I was in first grade. I picked up the phone and dialed—not Peter but Scott.

"Can you come over in about fifteen minutes?" I asked. "I promised to help my dad for a few minutes, but then I need your help."

"Sure," he said.

"And bring Peter Raskin's phone number," I added.

"I don't think I have it, but I'll check."

"You gotta have it," I pleaded before I hung up.

As I leaned forward the diary fell from under my arm. I picked it up, still thinking about Peter and boys in general. I wondered if boys kept diaries. (JohnBoy did on *The Waltons* TV show.)

Maybe my dad kept a diary. I wondered what he was like at thirteen, and if a girl had ever asked him out and what she said and what he said. I took a last gulp and wiped my milk mustache on a dish towel. I put the milk away, squashed the paper cup and tossed it in the garbage pail, then headed for the basement. Maybe Dad, too, would be able to help me. I kind of knew what I was going to do, but it wouldn't hurt to have another opinion about calling Peter . . . and I wondered if Dad knew anything about Mr. X. My reading about Mom and Mr. X would have to wait a bit.

I walked down the basement stairs, jumping the last two with a thump.

"Back here," Dad called. "I'll finish with Jillie in a minute and you're next."

I opened the door to the lab. Gray file cabinets were arranged in a U shape. They had wood platforms on top of them covered with different colored wires, electronic instruments, metal cases with drawers full of electronic parts like transistors, and stacks of papers. Dad could have worked in a fancy lab in Washington, but he wanted to work at home so he and Mom could both work and take care of the house and Jillie, Beth, and me. I'm glad about that. A lot of my friends' fathers are away on business trips more than they're home.

Jillie had this armband strapped to her upper arm like when the doctor takes your blood pressure. Dad was fiddling with some beeping, blinking equipment and watching the bionic hand open and close. This government research project was a tough one. I'd heard Dad say it's no easy job to imitate nature and make a hand for people who lost their own hands. I'd also heard him say if he didn't finish this project soon, he might lose this contract and future ones. Then how could he work at home?

Dad's glasses rested on top of his wavy blond hair. He looked even taller than he was because he was sitting on a high swivel chair, maneuvering it back and forth between Jillie and the table where his notebooks were spread out.

"You smell like brownies," Jillie said when I was close to her and Dad. "Everything smells like brownies." She looked at my father. "Except you. You always smell like shaving cream."

Dad unhooked the band on Jill's arm, helped her get down from the stool, and sent her off with a pat on her behind.

"Go on and enjoy your brownies. Take a big bite for me," he added and helped me up on the seat. The diary rested on my lap "Thanks for your help, Jillie," Dad said.

"Okay," Jillie answered. "I'll save a brownie specially for you." And she was on her way. Like a mouse entering a cheese factory, she followed the scent.

"Velcome to Transylvania," my father joked in his Count Dracula voice as he rolled up my sleeve and wrapped an elastic band around my arm. It had cold gook called electrode jelly on the five metal dots that pressed against my skin. I knew that they were electrodes and the jelly helped them pick up the electric signals my arm muscles send up to my skin. My dad had explained this to me a trillion times so I would at least know about his work. When I was younger and in kindergarten, a teacher asked me what kind of work my father did. I didn't understand then about engineers and inventing. I told her he plays in the basement all day.

"Open and close your fist," Dad directed. And I did, but my mind dreamed of Peter's hands around my waist as we danced to the closing song, "Stairway to Heaven."

On the table next to me lay the bionic hand, which was connected to wires that hung from my armband. When I opened my fist, the bionic hand opened. When I closed my fist, the hand closed.

"Great!" my father shouted. "It's even picking up your low signals. I'm getting there."

In spite of Dad's excitement, I didn't ask my usual

questions. All this bored me today. I had questions to ask, but they were about dates and dances and maybe Mr. X, not bionics.

Dad adjusted some knobs on his equipment. Lots of lights blinked across a screen and a static noise filled the air like when I'm between stations on my radio. I hate that sound. It made me wriggle, and the diary slipped off my lap and dropped.

"What's that?" Dad asked. He looked down at the red-leather book, then got off his seat. He bent down and picked up the diary for me.

"That's Mom at thirteen," I said, "and I think you better give her back to me. I don't know if I'm supposed to keep it private." I could tell from his thoughtful expression that he'd never seen this book before. I chickened out, deciding I was not going to be the one to introduce him to Mom's Mr. X.

"She sure was strange-looking, that Mom at thirteen, red and rectangular," Dad said.

Sometimes my dad is so silly. I shook my head. He flipped the pages, and I got this nervous feeling inside me, but then he closed the diary before he could read a line.

"What were you like at thirteen?" I asked, trying to get onto the important stuff about boys and girls and dances and away from the temptation of betraying Mom's confidence and asking Dad about Mr. X. "Were you ever cute?" I added.

"Yes!" he said indignantly. "Very cute! I still am." His high swivel chair squeaked as he leaned against the backrest. "I had a big pompadour, like a hill of hair over my forehead. I wasn't a fifties greaser, like in the movies. From what I remember, there were more clean-cut kids in the fifties than greasebombs. I had wavy hair and I was very, very nice."

"And not at all conceited?" I said.

Dad hugged me, wire connections, armbands, and all. I like to be hugged by my father.

Then he handed me Mom's diary.

"Do boys keep diaries?" I asked.

"I guess maybe some do. I didn't," he said.

"Don't men want to remember back to when they were boys?" I asked.

"Sure," he said. "Somewhere I've got this cigar box full of treasures, like old photos and a gold medal from the track team."

I guess men are sentimental too.

"I'll look for that cigar box later," Dad said. "I'd better get back to work now before I forget what I was experimenting with."

I hoped maybe he had photos of his girlfriends. Now, that would be interesting, and maybe he'd show them to Mom too, and she'd tell us all about whether Mr. X ever noticed her. That reminded me of phoning Peter, and I wondered where Scott was. He just had to have that phone number.

"When you were my age, were boys ever asked out by girls?" I said.

Dad rubbed his hands together like when you want to warm up after skating. "Girls," he answered, "—that was my favorite subject. In the yearbook they said I was like Bayer aspirin—I see a girl and go to work in two seconds—something like that. But really, Karen, I've got to get back to work now." Even though my dad jokes around sometimes, I know this project is very important to him. It's been very tough, but he's really close to finishing it.

"Okay, Dad, I get the hint. Time's up." I started to wiggle around on the stool, impatient to hear the doorbell. Where was Scott? Could you get lost only walking one block? This wasn't a blizzard! He better know Peter's number. I wanted to call Peter and get all this worrying over already. And if I found out Dana had already asked Peter to the dance . . . I didn't want to even think about that!

Finally the doorbell rang and I heard Scott's voice when Jill let him in. I started to go, but I was still wired to the bionic hand.

"Watch it, Karen." Dad spoke sharply. "Don't pull at the wires!"

"Sorry," I said. "Scott's here."

"He'll wait a minute," Dad said. "Go ahead, ask one more question while I unwire you."

"Okay. Did a girl ever ask you out?"

"Sure," Dad answered. "I think I've got a class picture with that old girlfriend in it."

"Can I see it later?" I asked. Somehow I couldn't picture my dad with anyone else but my mom. I didn't wait for him to answer. "I'm going to ask a boy out," I said. I spoke as if I really meant it. It even surprised me.

"Hey, Karen! I'm here!" Scott called downstairs. "Does your dad want me to help him?"

"I'll be right up," I called. If Scott came down here to help, I'd never get him upstairs. He loves to help my dad. But today I needed his help to make my phone call. Time was running out. I was still wired up.

"And what boy are you asking out?" Dad said. "And where are you going? And when?" he added as he unhooked my armband, freeing me to go upstairs—almost. He kind of hung onto my hand.

Yes. My dad was treating me like a baby again. I liked it better when he was answering questions rather than asking them, and right now I wished he would let go of my hand.

"Karen!" Scott called again.

"Gotta go," I said. "The boy's name is Peter and the dance is Thursday night because there's no school Friday. It's a teacher in-service training day. I'll tell you the rest later."

As I went out of the lab Dad called, "I'll find that memory box. Thanks for your helping hand, ha-ha-ha," he said, adding the latest of his series of bionic hand jokes. "And, Karen," he called in a serious voice, "I hope I was of some help to you too."

"You were, Dad," I said, and I meant it.

"Oh," Dad added in his regular voice, "I want to meet that boy before you go out with him."

"He didn't even say yes yet," I called as I started up the stairs. "I haven't even phoned him."

"He couldn't possibly refuse someone as lovely as you," my dad shouted. "Someone who's not only lovely but also has a good head on her shoulders."

Even though I like them, sometimes I get embarrassed by compliments, so I turn them into jokes. "I may have a good head on my shoulders," I said, "but I'd forget it if it wasn't attached."

I could hear my dad's laughter as I walked up the stairs and it made me feel good. It was probably a joke only a father would think funny—my father. I wish my sense of humor was appreciated outside my family, as well.

"Karen," Scott called down again.

"I'm coming," I called back. Then I crossed my fingers for luck and raced up the stairs, shouting, "Did you find Peter's number?"

5

Ma and Pa Bell Against Me

I closed the basement door behind me so Dad wouldn't hear "upstairs noise," as he calls it. I walked into the kitchen, still clutching Mom's diary.

Scott and Jillie were sitting at the kitchen table eating brownies. Jillie obviously had done the serving—a trail of brownie crumbs led the way across the white bricklike floor from the counter to the table. Jillie would be great in a starring role in *Hansel and Gretel*.

"Hi, Scott. Did you bring Peter's number? I couldn't find it listed in the phone book so I sure hope you know it."

"I haven't been friends with Peter since Boy Scouts a couple of years ago," Scott answered, and my hopes faded like sky writing. "I don't have his number anywhere—sorry."

"But don't you have some old address- and phone-number book?" I asked. "I know I still have mine from kindergarten."

"Some people do throw things out, Karen," Scott said.

I didn't even sit down. "Finish chewing your brownie quickly. We've got business to take care of."

"I wanna help," Jillie begged.

The way I was feeling, I wished she could find the number, call, and ask Peter to the dance for me. No one can refuse Jillie's little voice. I was beginning to wish I were five again. Everything was so simple then. I was always so good at saying, "Can you come out and play with me?" Who cared then if it was a boy or a girl or who asked who? So why was asking Peter to the dance so tough now? Why? I asked myself again, and answered, "Because if he says no, I'll die. It's as simple as that."

"Let me help with your business like I help Daddy," Jill said, interrupting my thoughts, poking her finger in my arm.

I always give in to Jillie's demands. Sometimes I get angry, but I give in anyway because she's the "baby." I handed her the diary and told her she could help first by putting this red-leather book on the desk in my room and then she could spray-clean the kitchen table. It would keep her busy and happy drawing stick figures with her finger-tip, the way our grandma had once shown her. Then, with a paper towel, she'd be even busier erasing those round smiling faces and spiderlike legs. Jillie delivered the diary and was back in a flash. I took the Windex from the cabinet and handed it to her. Then I handed Scott the slip of paper I had stuck in the phone book. I wished it had Peter's number on it and not just Lori's. I also wished that I'd already asked Peter to the dance the way Lori had already asked Scott.

"Here's Lori's number," I said.

Scott walked over to the kitchen desk and pointed to the phone. "It's a good thing I ate the brownies already or I'd lose my appetite," he teased.

I tried not to worry about how I'd ever get Peter's number. I waited to hear if Scott would say yes or no to

Lori's dance invitation. I think it took him longer to push the buttons than to talk. He didn't even sit down.

"Hello, Lori? This is Scott. . . . Yeah . . . I'll go. . . . See ya." Scott hung up the phone. "Whew! That's over!" he said and collapsed dramatically in a heap on the floor.

"I never knew boys get so nervous about calling a girl," I said.

"I don't know about all boys, but *I* sure get nervous," Scott admitted.

I sat down on the floor next to him. We leaned against the refrigerator door.

"If you listen to TV," he said, "you think boys are made of steel. I think it's more like we're made of aluminum foil."

"Girls too," I said.

Scott smiled and gave me a little push as I struggled to get up. "I'll call Ma Bell," I said, "and see if maybe Peter got a new number or something. Our phone book's from last year. Maybe his number is listed after all."

My father always calls the phone company "Ma Bell." I'm not sure why. Maybe because it's usually a woman's voice at information. But I knew he'd have to change the name when a deep man's voice said, "Operator two-nine-seven—what city please?"

"Uh, Hillsboro," I said and cleared my throat. "On Falcon Court, the name is Raskin. I don't know the first name," I mumbled.

"Hold on, please. Let me check."

Covering the mouthpiece with the palm of my hand, I whispered to Scott, "Make it Pa Bell—it's a male operator."

"Equality at last," Scott said, sounding a lot like his mom.

"Still checking, Ms. One moment, please."

"Can I help more?" Jillie begged, tugging at my sleeve, ready to get into the act.

"Sorry to keep you waiting," the operator said. "There is no Raskin listed in Hillsboro. I have a Mr. Raskin in Belle Mead."

"No. That's not it," I said as Jillie continued to tug.

"I have a Raskin Exterminators in Montgomery."

"No. This Raskin is in Hillsboro," I said, trying to concentrate while Jillie wound herself around the telephone cord.

"Why didn't you use your phone book?" the operator asked, as if I were guilty of laziness or something.

"I did look in the phone book. But the number's not listed. Is it an unlisted number?" I figured it could just be a mistake, that it was left out of the book.

"Hold on, I'm looking," the deep voice sang.

"He's still looking," I told Scott and Jillie.

"Where is he looking?" Scott laughed. "Afghanistan?"

"Karen, I wanna help!" Jillie tugged at my vest. My grandma named her "the cutest nudge in the world." Sometimes, like now, I'm not so sure about "cute."

"Ssh," I said. "Be quiet now, for just one more minute."

"But Nancy, in my class, has the same name," Jillie shouted. Jillie is the kind of kid who all of a sudden tells you about something that has nothing to do with anything. I have learned to tune her out.

"Yes, ma'am, the Raskins' number is unlisted," the operator finally said. "We cannot give it out."

"Oh, please," I begged, untwisting the knots that Jillie had made in the phone cord. "You could tell me, I'm a friend of the Raskins."

"Sorry, ma'am, it's against regulations."

"But it's an emergency," I blurted out. To me it was, so I wasn't lying. And when Jillie whined, "I want to HEL-L-L-P!" I decided to let her, and I put the phone near her mouth on the last word.

Sometimes Scott and I don't need words to talk to each other. He caught on and created an instant agony scene. "Get that Raskin telephone number quick!" he shouted. "We've got to get through to them before the ambulance comes." Then, in a totally different voice, he cried, "Oh no! What will we do? How will we get the number?" Next he did his best siren imitation, throwing his voice so it sounded like the siren was coming closer and closer.

Jillie got caught up in the game and yelled, "I'll get the number," and dashed off.

"I'll connect you with my supervisor," the operator said.

"I'm sorry," a woman said, getting on the line, "we cannot give out an unlisted number. If it is an emergency, I will connect you with the police. Perhaps they can help."

Ma Bell had me there. "Uh, thanks anyway," I said and hung up. "It's a lost cause," I moaned and sank down onto the floor. "Peter might as well be on the moon. It's no use. I just won't go to the dance, that's all."

Scott put his hand on my shoulder and looked me straight in the eye. "I think you're glad you can't find the number. It's a good excuse."

"You're right," I said, wishing I didn't really need someone else pushing me to do what I should do on my own. "A little bird is not going to tell me the number. I may have to call every kid I know in school. Someone's got to have Peter's number."

"Way to go, Karen." Scott cheered like at a softball game.

My grandmother once told me that when I can't find any answer, to close my eyes like window shades pulled down, and then open them and take another look and I might find the answer. I did it.

Only all I found when I opened my eyes was Jillie interrupting us. She slid back into the kitchen like a cartoon character slides to the edge of a cliff and stops short. Jillie hates shoes and never wears them inside the house. She loves to slide in her socks. She was waving this mimeographed sheet of names and addresses and phone numbers.

"I got it," she said, smiling and still playing. "Make the siren noise again, Scott," she pleaded.

I was in no mood for my sister at five and her pretend world. I had serious troubles. How could you phone a boy if you didn't have his telephone number?

"Go play or something, Jillie, okay?" I ordered rather than asked.

She just waved the sheet of paper more and more and closer and closer till it was flapping in my face. "I got it from Mommy, just now." She whined the last word like a real crybaby.

Before I knew it, my temper was flaring. "Enough!" I yelled. "Enough pestering!" I grabbed the paper she was still waving in my face and crumpled it up. Then I threw it, hitting her on the arm, just a light tap. But her eyes welled up with tears. "That didn't hurt you. What are you crying about!" I yelled, getting even angrier.

Scott hugged Jillie, and I felt like the wicked witch in the fairy tales I read her.

"You don't have to scare the kid to death," Scott said, patting Jillie on the head, trying to get her to stop crying. Then he bent down and picked up the crumpled ball of paper and opened it. He smoothed it out on the table. I looked over his shoulder, pretending to read Jillie's paper, to soothe her, when a name on it caught my attention.

"Scott! You won't believe this!" I shouted and waved the paper at him. Then I sat down on the kitchen chair, pulled Jillie onto my lap, and gave her the biggest hug and kiss.

Jillie can turn off tears as fast as she can turn them on, and a kiss works like magic.

"Look at this, Scott," I said. I was still waving the paper. "Jillie was the biggest help of all."

She beamed at my praise as if she'd just whistled for the first time!

"I helped?" Jillie asked. "I really helped you?"

"Let me see," Scott said. "Hold the paper still."

I pointed to the name and number. "Nancy Raskin, that's Peter's little sister. The class mother's got to have even unlisted telephone numbers in case there's an emergency closing. Dad's my class 'mother,' and Mom's Jillie's."

"Nancy's my friend in school," Jillie said. "I told you before that she has the same name you keep yelling. Nancy and I trade snacks. She always has cookies with sprinkles on top."

"Good girl," Scott said, and he lifted Jillie and swung her around. Then he sent her off to her room to draw twenty dogs. "Go on, Karen," Scott ordered. "Call Peter—right now!"

For a moment I felt as free as on the last day of school. I had the number now—today! I lifted up the phone, then hung it up again. A feeling of dread took over. Suddenly I was scared. We'd learned in science that our bodies are 80 percent liquid. And I felt like all the fluid in my body had ripples. "What if Peter says no?" I asked. "What if he laughs at me and says, 'You? Ha!' What if his mother or father answers?"

"Go on. Call," Scott said. He picked up the phone and handed it to me. "If his mother or father answers, imitate that operator like you did before. Say, 'This is Andrew. Is Peter there?' Peter's not gonna want his parents to know a girl called. They always think it's so cute."

I dialed, then listened breathlessly as the phone rang three times at the other end. My luck—no one would be home. Then I heard this deep voice. I thought I would never be able to make another sound.

"Hello," I finally said, making my own voice sound low-pitched. "This is Andrew. Is Peter there?" I almost fainted when the voice crackled and got higher and said, "This *is* Peter."

For a minute he'd sounded so grown-up. If I hung up quickly and called back, he'd still know it was me and I'd feel like a real durf. I looked up at Scott for confidence and remembered how he'd once told me that boys like honesty, so I blurted out, all in one breath, "This is Karen, I thought you were your father, you sound so much older on the phone." I wished Peter would say something, but he didn't, so I went on. "I called to ask you to the"—I took a deep breath so I wouldn't faint for sure, then I said the rest—"Sadie Hawkins Day Winter Switch Dance," even though just saying, "school dance" would have been enough.

I breathed such a sigh of relief at letting the question out that I almost didn't hear the answer. At least he hadn't laughed. And he hadn't said no. Only he hadn't said yes either.

Peter cleared his throat. "I'll let you know in math tomorrow," he said. "Okay?"

All I could say was, "Okay. Bye," and I hung up.

"What did he say?" Scott asked.

"I did it! I did it! I called Peter!" I opened and closed the silverware drawer for no reason other than excitement. "He told me, 'I'll let you know in math, tomorrow, okay?' "

"He probably has to ask his parents. He can't tell you that." Scott was interpreting Peter's words.

"Or maybe he's considering another offer. I am not good at waiting for someone else to procrastinate," I added and collapsed into a chair.

"So what's one more day when there are still brownies to eat?" Scott said, taking one for himself. "Want one to celebrate asking Peter?"

I wasn't quite ready to celebrate in advance and my stomach felt like a roller disco. To me it seemed like tomorrow, and Peter's answer, were two months away, at least—and I still had to get the tickets from Joey Dillon. This was one time I didn't want to put things off.

6

Answers and More Questions

I jumped to answer when the phone rang, dreaming it was Peter calling back to say yes—or no—but it was only Scott's mom. She's an accountant, and she'd been working in New York all day. She was on her way home but would be a bit late because of the snow. "I figured Scott would be at your house if he wasn't at home," she said. "Could he stay for dinner?" I asked Mom and she said yes.

Dad took Jill and went to pick up Beth at her friend Cheryl's. Scott and I made the salad, munching on the carrot slices that seemed to fly off the cutting board. By the time Dad, Beth, and Jillie returned, Scott and I had finished making this beautiful salad. It even had a radish on top cut like a flower (with a few missing petals).

"Hi," Beth greeted in the sweetest voice, and even set the table without a fuss. She also made sure she sat next to Scott.

By dinner time I could hear the whirring of snowplows clearing the roads. Usually I think Hillsboro Township's road crew is so efficient it's disgusting, doing us hardworking kids out of an extra snowday. But tonight, for the first time in my life, I was wishing we wouldn't have a snowday.

I had to be at school tomorrow to find out Peter's answer.

"The snow's so white," Mom said, looking out the window next to the table as she spooned steaming pot roast and noodles from the pan to our plates.

"Till I moved out of the city," Dad said, laughing, "I always thought snow was gray with occasional yellow spots. Air pollution and pet pollution," he added.

"Jillie, don't squash the noodles onto the table, please," Mom said.

Scott winked at Jillie, and she spent the rest of the mealtime practicing winking. Beth stared at Scott and hardly ate a bite. I think she's starting to like boys, and Scott's her first crush. I'm not sure I like that idea.

Afterward, as usual, we all cleared our own places at the table, and Scott helped my dad load the dishwasher. A car horn honked out front. "Scott's mom's here to pick him up," Jillie announced after racing to look out the window. Scott's dad is usually too busy taking care of his patients at the hospital to help out with driving, like my dad does.

I helped Scott on with his jacket.

"What are you doing?" he said, twisting around.

He was having trouble finding the sleeve. That always happens to me when someone helps me on with my jacket. I suddenly feel like I have three arms and there's no armhole in the jacket at all.

"Bye," I called as Scott went out and Mom closed the door behind him.

I was in my room finishing up my English assignment. I really got carried away writing that letter "evoking emotion." Then I listened to the ten-thirty weather report on the radio, and was deciding what to wear to school the next day when World War III began. "Beth," I called, "where is my blue sweater? The one you borrowed last week."

"It's in my room," she called back.

"Could you bring it to me?" I asked.

"No!" she yelled back. "Come get it."

"You borrowed it," I shouted. "You return it to my room."

"Girls!" my father yelled. "Cut out that arguing. I'm trying to listen to this science special on TV. I can't even hear myself think." His words didn't help one bit; our fight went on.

Then Mom called out her latest psychological solution. "I read an article that said 'Try bantering—instead of bickering.' At least it expands your mind. But how about doing it where I don't have to listen to it!"

"You're never borrowing anything of mine again, and that's final," I yelled to Beth and kicked my door shut. Then I picked up my memo book and wrote:

> *MEMO: To myself when I have two teenage daughters. I will leave them alone and let them fight.*

The evening dragged on. I phoned Allison. Allison phoned me. I watched a bit of the science special with Dad. It was about laser beams, one of my favorite subjects. But tonight I was so restless and worried, I decided to clean my room. Now, that's really the pits.

The evening may have dragged on, but the night was even worse. It seemed endless. I wanted to read Mom's diary, but I couldn't find where Jillie had put it. From my bed I heard every tick of the clock. I felt every wrinkle in my sheets. I could even hear my parakeet, Bruno, breathe. Everything kept me up. By the time I saw Peter in math the next day and found out his answer, I'd have big black circles under my eyes. Then he'd surely say no. No one wants to go to a dance with a raccoon!

I heard my dad laugh at the *Johnny Carson Show*. I even heard Jillie grinding her teeth and Beth telling her to stop it or she'd be toothless by age seven. I heard the TV click off. I heard water running in the shower and a toilet flushing. Soon I heard snoring from my parents' bedroom even though they both always deny that they snore.

It was no use. Every time I closed my eyes I imagined I heard Peter saying no. Finally I got up and turned on the light. I searched the room to find Mom's diary. If I was going to be wide awake, I might as well do something interesting. With all this business about Peter, there'd been no chance to read more of the diary until now.

How could a red-leather diary disappear? I searched my room again. No diary. I'd told Jillie to put it on my desk. So where was it? Could Beth have found it? I was about to go into her room and wake her up when I finally spotted the diary way back on my desk, under my dictionary with its red-leatherlike cover. In my mind I'd wrongly accused Beth. Why? When we were little, we'd trusted each other so much. What was happening to us? I felt sad.

I took out my flashlight and shut off the ceiling light. Then, clutching Mom's diary, I curled back up in my bed to thumb through the pages.

May 16, 1955
Today the club went to the ball game. It was a double-header at Ebbets Field. It was between the Brooklyn Dodgers and the Cincinnati Reds. In the first game the Dodgers won 4-2 because Hodges hit a GRAND SLAM! YEAH DODGERS!

Mom knew about grand slams? At my softball game she claps when someone catches the ball, even though that means an out for my team. And when I watch the Mets' game on TV she always asks "What's happening?"

> April 30, 1955
> *Today I went with Sheila and Elayne to Coney Island.*
> *I went on the Virginia Reel. On it the cars turn all*
> *around and you go up and down and around curves*
> *very fast. I nearly fell out. We went on a swinging car*
> *on the Wonderwheel and others. Guess who I saw*
> *eating hot dogs at Nathan's? Mr. X, but he wasn't*
> *alone.*

Did she say anything to him anyway? And who was he with? I wished she'd written more. And is this the same mother who avoids Great Adventure like the plague? Went alone with just friends, not parents? She'd never let me go alone.

For some reason, while I was reading about Mom at thirteen, it felt like when you first put calamine lotion on a mosquito bite. For the moment the itch was gone. My mind was off Peter. But before I even closed the diary and turned out my flashlight, I felt uncomfortable again, so I kept on reading. I was glad I did.

> January 13, 1955
> *Today the most embarrassing thing happened to me. I*
> *was walking up the stairs when the slit in my skirt*
> *ripped up to my thigh. Two boys were walking behind*
> *me and they were laughing, probably at me. I thought*
> *I'd die. I ran to the homemaking room and Miss Ma-*
> *gee gave me a needle and thread. I had to sit behind a*

screen, in my slip. I sewed the skirt, but what a mess.
I hope that never happens again.

That sounded like something that could easily happen to
me, especially since slit skirts are in style now too. I would
definitely not wear a slit skirt to the dance if Peter said yes.
"Thanks, Ma, for saving me an embarrassing moment," I
whispered to the diary.

I couldn't help laughing at the next one.

February 16, 1955
In French I made a mistake on the blackboard, so the
translation read "My neighbors are bigger than your
pears." Everyone laughed.

Poor Mom. I would have died on the spot, and she lived
to have children of her own.

This stuff was good, but I wanted to know more about
Mr. X. Then I found:

March 18, 1955
The club party was terrific. Mr. X lives in the same
apartment building as my friend Sheila, where the
party was. I rode up in the elevator with him. I even
spoke to him. I said, "Third floor, please." I wish he
were younger or I were older. Boys my age are such
babies. They were so silly—throwing M&M's, trying
to get them to go down the girls' blouses. I had fun
anyway. The girls all sat in a corner making up droo-
dles and the boys had to guess them. I liked this one.
What's this?

A navel orange wearing a bikini.

Maybe I considered that a happy ending. She had fun. Or I guess I finally just conked out, because in the morning the diary and a very dim flashlight, still on, were next to me in my bed.

I didn't feel like talking to anyone. For the first time I didn't want anyone telling me it would all work out. I got up and checked the radio for any school closings. Bless the Hillsboro road crews—there was school today. I dressed early, before Beth took up residence in the bathroom. For breakfast I ate some Alpha-Bits. That was a mistake. My bowl of cereal seemed like a crystal ball answering the question pounding in my head: What will Peter say? And the miserable Alpha-Bits kept spelling out NO! There didn't seem to be a letter *Y* in the entire box.

I dumped the cereal and ate a leftover brownie. I brushed my teeth, checking in the mirror to make sure I didn't have a dark spot of chocolate caught in my braces or between my front teeth.

"Karen, I have to get into the bathroom!" Beth howled, pounding on the door.

"You mean you don't like to wait?" I answered, taking my time, the way Beth always does.

"You don't make Jillie wait," Beth said. "You always let her right in."

"So do you," I said. It's hard to believe it now, but when we were little, before Jillie was old enough to walk, Beth and I didn't fight over the bathroom. We even took showers together. Things sure change.

Before I left the house, warmly dressed but bootless of course, I ran back to my room to feed Bruno and fill the feeder for the outside birds. I also wrote:

> *MEMO: To myself when I have children. I will have only two.*

I also grabbed a piece of bread from the kitchen counter, and as I walked to the bus stop I crumbled up the bread and tossed it on the snow. I was so busy sprinkling bread and watching the hungry birds come and get it that I bumped right into the old man as he walked by. I was a little early this morning—as I'd hoped to be—in time to meet him on his usual schedule.

"Sorry," I said. He kind of bowed to me and said something that sounded like "Nice girl," then "What's your name?" And I muttered "Karen."

"Nice girl, Karen," he said, then started to walk on.

"You like birds?" I called after him. That's all I could think of to say.

"Birds are beautiful," he called back.

"And hungry," I said, pointing to the birds who were nibbling the crumbs I'd dropped.

"Yes. But they won't starve with Karen and me around. Right?" The man laughed, waved, and walked on.

He seemed to walk slower today. I wished I had asked him where he walks to, and why he looks at my house every day. But I was shy. Well, at least I'd met him—or rather, he'd met me. I should have asked him his name. He knew mine now. I watched him walk on. I wanted to call to him and talk some more, but I couldn't just call, "Hey, man!," so I walked to the bus stop.

7

Announcements

I knew Peter well enough to know that he wouldn't give me an answer at the bus stop—not with Dana around. But maybe he'd get there early too. That's what I planned to do anyway.

The snow crunched as I walked, but it was frozen and I didn't sink in. I had to squint my eyes to see. The sun bounced off that white snow looking like a scene on a TV that has no contrast control.

I waited, slowly turning into an ice statue. Scott arrived and we talked, but Peter not only didn't arrive first, he didn't arrive second, third, or fourth. I began to worry. Was he going to be absent? Some other kids started throwing snowballs. I don't mind snowballs of fresh, soft snow. But old ones with hard ice are not for me. I put my books up for protection. Some of my papers fell out and I had to chase them in the wind.

Finally, just as the bus skidded around the corner, so did Peter. He was last, or next to last, because he arrived with Dana at his side, just in time to climb into the bus. As he passed my seat he didn't even look at me. Not a good sign for one hoping for the answer "Yes, I'll go to the dance." I felt a sinking feeling in my stomach. As the bus swerved and bumped its usual way, Scott leaned across the aisle and whispered.

"Don't worry, Karen," he explained. "You'll probably get the tickets from Joey Dillon, and Peter probably has to work up to answering yes. Boys don't like to give answers like that when other kids are around."

"Why? Girls are proud to be asked out," I said. "But, anyway, he could have at least smiled at me . . . unless . . . he's thinking up a way to break the bad news. And what do you mean, I'll probably get the tickets from Joey Dillon? You weren't talking 'probably' yesterday. You were saying 'of course' and 'sure.' "

At that thought I felt like we'd just gone over this enormous bump, even though we hadn't.

Then Scott added loudly, "Give me back that pencil, you durf," pretending I'd grabbed his pencil and he'd leaned over to get it back.

I caught on and quickly gave him one of my pencils. Sometimes I wonder why we can't just be friends in front of everyone.

When the bus swerved around the last turn, a snowball seemed to come out of nowhere and smash against the windshield.

"*Bleep bleep* kids with their *bleep bleep* snowballs!" The bus driver blew the horn to drown out each curse. "That's so dangerous."

All the kids started filling in the bleeps.

The bus parked in front of school and we jumped off like a busload of kangaroos. Scott raced to find Lori, and Dana ran to greet her friend Gwen. I walked slowly, hoping Peter, with his long legs and track team experience, would catch up and tell me how he'd love to go to the dance with me. How he's liked me for months—or at least mutter "Yes." Allison was with Jeff, so I didn't bother her.

Then a shower of snow gently sprinkled down on me from Peter's extended hand, and he said, not the words I'd hoped for, but at least not the words I'd dreaded. He just called his usual words as I stared up at his dark hair and blue eyes—"See ya in math"—and he took off inside.

As I got to the door I could hear the shrieks and thuds as a snowball fight was starting behind me. A couple of kids from the sixth grade hid behind a tree and threw snowballs at cars driving on the side road.

I didn't brush the snow from my hair. After all, Peter had put it there.

I felt excited and full of energy, and I made a snowball of my own just to toss in the air. I threw it as high as I could. Then I ducked inside, not looking to see if or where it landed.

I met Allison at our locker. I had nothing new to tell her since our four phone conversations the night before, but she was full of news about "Jeff this and Jeff that."

We had a sub for homeroom, which is always a riot. I took one look and had her figured out. This was one of those old-fashioned subs who shake and say, "Do anything. Just be good." The kind of person who looks like she'll break. I love to hear subs mispronounce names, so I listened carefully.

"Anthony Bennotti?" she called, perfectly.

I figured she must know his mother or something.

"Barbara Dennis?"

"Here."

No mistake, yet . . . Then she called, "Michelle Dubin?"

And everyone cracked up. We all twisted in our seats to face the person in question.

"Answer her, Michelle," Jeff teased, making his voice high-sounding.

And then this big kid, Michael Dubin, said "HERE!" in a deep voice. "Michael, not Michelle." And under his breath he added, "What kind of teacher is she anyway? Can't she even read?"

We giggled, and some kids snorted or whistled. Then a note was passed around and at the same time all of us clicked our ball-point pens.

The loudspeaker blasted, and the everyday voice, sounding more frantic than usual, read a list of names, announcing, "These people are to report to the principal's office—*immediately*."

It reminded me of Monopoly. I almost expected her to say, "Do not pass Go. Do not collect two hundred dollars." It did sound like trouble was brewing. I wasn't paying much attention to the announcements. I was scribbling Peter and Karen on the inside of my book cover. So I was really startled when the last name announced was mine. I got a chill when I heard it. I also got embarrassed. Kids teasingly said, "Karen? *You're* in trouble?" And Allison was looking at me questioningly.

I had never been called down to the principal's office in my life. So I couldn't imagine why he wanted to see me now. But worse yet, how could I go to the principal's office when my next class was math? At the bus stop yesterday I'd promised to check Peter's math paper right before class, only the class had been canceled when we were sent home early. But most important, I had to go to math to find out Peter's answer to my invitation. With all those names just announced, it would be a long wait in the office. I had to decide what to do. I couldn't just ignore a call to the principal's office. I'd just have to try to make it a quick trip and be out in time for math. Only I was walking slowly while I was figuring all this out, wondering why he wanted to see me. By the time I got there I was last on line.

It was standing-room-only with all the kids that had been sent for. But they were kids who were often in trouble. Why was I here? I waited nervously, twisting a tissue I'd found in my pocket. Everyone was silent, even the kids who are usually loud. The only noise was of typing and dialing phones and the secretary's gravelly voice.

No one seemed to come out of the principal's inner office. Maybe there was another door?

I was finally seated on the hard wooden bench, with only four kids ahead of me, when the bell rang for changing classes. The gravel-voiced secretary cleared her throat but sounded the same as she said, "You."

"Me?" I said, looking around.

"Yes, you," she repeated.

I shivered and got up, surprised to be going ahead of the four others and scared to death.

Then she pointed, not to the principal's door but to the door to the hall, and said, "Come back in fifteen minutes. No sense sitting here all day."

With a sigh of relief I raced off to math. I hoped Peter hadn't heard my name on the P.A. system. Before math he's usually busy in the Media Center closet getting the day's projectors and films ready. He's president of the Audio-Visual Squad. Sometimes he's even late for math if he has to deliver a projector.

Sure enough, I made it to class before he did. I had also totally chewed up one pencil by the time Peter sat down next to me. If he said no, I prayed I wouldn't start to cry and make a fool of myself—although at least I wouldn't have to worry about getting tickets from Joey Dillon. And if he said yes (I crossed my fingers under the desk), I didn't know what I'd say or do. I did a lot of hoping while I waited for Peter to speak. Oh, please say yes, I wished.

But I thought I would pass out altogether when Peter gave me his paper to check, and not only didn't mention my being called down to the office but patted my head. Usually he just taps me on the head with his pencil. "Your hair's still wet," he said, and he pushed a damp strand out of my eyes. "Hey, Andrew," he whispered and winked to me, using the name I'd used when I phoned him the day before. Then he laughed and added, "What time are we going to the dance tomorrow night?"

I think I took a deep breath, closed my eyes, and mumbled "Seven-thirty." Then I quickly took his paper and showed him where he'd reversed his numbers and had written 658 meters for the answer to Problem D, instead of 568. "You did it right. You just switched the numbers around in your answer," I explained. Peter is really smart when he's figuring out problems, but he gets the numbers mixed up when he writes them down.

"I get it," he said.

I knew I would never think of another thing to say. I was literally saved by, not the bell, as the saying goes, but by sirens. An ambulance pulled up to the school just as Mr. Corn, our teacher, walked into the room carrying a stack of books.

"You may *walk* to the window and take a look. Then sit down and we'll talk about what's happening," Mr. Corn said, organizing our rush to the window.

A stretcher was rolled out of the ambulance and into the school. Kids shouted out possibilities.

"Mrs. H must have screamed so loud she had a stroke," this boy, John, suggested.

"Mr. Strab must have carried out his daily threat to chew up a kid and spit him out the window and he's choking on a bone," Maureen said.

"Nah," Peter added. "The lunchroom lady tasted today's school lunch."

"Enough of that joking." Mr. Corn brought us back to order.

"Maybe a kid is hurt?" someone else said, and we stopped joking and discussed who it might be.

The stretcher was wheeled back out, practically under our window. When I saw who was on it I was speechless. It was the green wool hat that caught my attention, and the crooked stick placed next to the old man on the stretcher. We watched the ambulance speed away and I got this empty feeling. I actually felt like they were taking away a friend, although I didn't even know his name. What was the old man doing at school, I wondered. I also had to get to the principal's office soon or they'd announce my name on the intercom *again!*

8

Everything Snowballs

I'm always very talkative to Peter in math. Today I couldn't even form a vowel. I also was trying to figure out how to leave this class and go to the principal's office without explaining why, when I didn't know why.

The teacher got our attention back on math by insisting we all do this problem he'd made up about the mileage to the hospital, calculating how fast the ambulance travels. My thoughts had wandered briefly to that hurt old man when Peter tapped my shoulder and once again took over the thinking space in my mind.

"Karen, help me write the example so I won't mess up," Peter whispered.

I looked at my watch. Fifteen minutes were almost up. It was nearly time for me to go to the principal's office. But how could I say no to Peter? Of course I knew going to the principal's office was more important, but it would only take a minute to help Peter. And after all, he'd just made plans to go to the dance with me. I couldn't say no to him now. Whenever I write the examples for Peter he gets them right, but if he writes them himself, he usually reverses the numbers and gets the wrong answers.

I leaned over and wrote the numbers down for him. We both came up with the answer at the same time and it was the same one.

"Brilliant," Peter said. "We're absolutely brilliant."

I'd gotten myself together and was about to tell Peter that we'd car-pool with Scott and Lori for the dance, and kind of slip in that I had to go to the office, when the loudspeaker crackled.

Oh no, I thought. The announcer's going to say, "Karen Berman to the principal's office *immediately*." And I'll die.

"Attention please," the voice boomed. "Some irresponsible young people were throwing snowballs at passing cars, and many of you have just witnessed the results. An innocent victim, an elderly man, was walking down the street and was hit by snowballs. He chased the trouble-makers. Unfortunately the man collapsed just as he got to the school building. The excitement may have been the cause. We do not know how grave his condition is. Those young people are in serious trouble now. Teachers are to discuss the matter further with their students." Click! The intercom went off.

That poor old man. How bad was his condition? Did he fall or faint—or have a heart attack? My imagination was taking over.

Then the intercom went back on and growled, "Karen Berman to the office immediately." Just as I'd dreaded. I turned very red and the pencil dropped out of my hand.

"Karen, you'd better go to the office right away," said Mr. Corn, and added, "You weren't involved in this, were you?" Peter and the entire class looked at me, waiting for an answer. How embarrassing!

"No," I said, kind of sinking into my seat.

"Snowballs are no joke," Mr. Corn said. "That man could

even have had a heart attack." Mr. Corn wasn't lecturing us, just leveling and letting us talk about it to each other or to him.

"I never thought of snowballs as causing an accident, before," Peter said.

"Me either," I agreed.

"I won't see you on the bus. I have a swim meet. I'll phone you later," Peter said. "What's your number?"

I told him, and he wrote it down. Then we raced out of the classroom.

"Good luck with the principal," he called after me.

I'd never gotten a phone call from any boy except Scott, and that's different. I would have been floating with joy if I wasn't on my way to the principal's office. I felt like someone had just gotten off my foot. Still in pain—but less of it.

I was almost there when I spotted Joey Dillon. He kind of blended into the crowd of kids who'd been rehearsing for a play in the all-purpose room. He's always selling something. Last year he sold beaded necklaces from his uncle's store. This year he's selling pens that smell like fruit when you write. But today I knew—as usual when there was a dance—that he'd be selling tickets. On Broadway I think they call it scalping, selling hard-to-get tickets at a higher price. And tickets were what I needed—very badly. I couldn't believe this was me doing this—buying tickets illegally on my way to the principal's office for God knows what reason.

I walked over to Joey Dillon. "I'll take two," I said.

"Meet me in the hall after seventh period," he said, walking away as Mr. Bush, the assistant principal, passed near us. That's Joey for you. He didn't panic. Instead he just blended in, ran after Mr. Bush, calling, "Want to buy a pen, Mr. Bush? I got a blueberry and a lemon left."

I headed for the principal's office. At least I'd solved one problem myself—getting the tickets. I felt kind of good. Maybe talking to the principal wouldn't be so bad either. Maybe he had something nice to tell me. I was really curious about why I'd been asked to speak to him at all.

When I got to the office, who should be sitting there but Dana.

"Caught smoking a grit in the john," she whispered to me. "I'm supposed to sit here until I air out and wait for the principal to get back."

Then I was told by the secretary in her loud gravel voice that Mr. Standish had been called out unexpectedly and I should come back after seventh period. What a run-around—and after seventh period was when I had to meet Joey Dillon.

In science we dissected a worm—and wouldn't you know it, for lunch we had spaghetti! I couldn't eat. I'd hoped Peter would sit with me in lunch, but he didn't. He sat with Dana, and I sat with Scott and Allison, Lori and Jeff.

"Peter said yes, sort of!" I announced. "I mean, in math he asked what time we're going to the dance, so it must be yes." I was practically suffocated as my friends crowded around me and patted my back. But then they started to ask why the principal wanted to see me. And then Dana walked by.

"Hey, Karen," she said, "you see the damn principal yet? He's lookin' for ya." And she smiled in a way that meant trouble.

Lots of kids were talking about the man who'd collapsed, and the snowballs, and how neat the ambulance was. Each kid I heard made the accident sound worse than the kid before.

On the ice cream line I heard Dana say, "I saw the whole thing. His face was turning blue and he was grabbing at his heart."

"The guy broke his leg in three places. I saw the bone sticking through the skin. It was totally disgusting—a puddle of blood," Gwen added. And everyone in line pretended to gag.

"You weren't even there, Gwen," Jeff said. "All I saw was that he was real pale and very still."

A lot of kids felt bad for the guy. Most of us just tease each other with snowballs. We don't throw them at cars and people.

That's why we were so shocked in seventh period when the loudspeaker boomed disaster in its grating voice. "Attention please. Because of the irresponsible incident with the snowballs, involving seventh graders, the Sadie Hawkins Day Winter Switch Dance has been canceled."

The kids showed their disappointment with deep breathing, sighing, and groaning sounds, and it made me think of those Saturday cartoons Jillie watches. The ones where buildings tremble and the sides get sucked in. There was the sound of fists banging on desks, pencils being broken in half, and papers being torn up and thrown into the air. Books were slammed closed. One word could be heard in every classroom—"UNFAIR!"

I was furious. I finally ask a boy. He says yes. He even writes down my phone number and says, "I'll call you later." I even arrange to get tickets illegally. And they cancel the dance! Plus, to make matters worse, I still had to go to the principal's office.

On a scale of one to ten, today was a negative number.

Between seventh and eighth periods a lot of kids were standing in the hall complaining about the dance being canceled. I looked around, trying to find Scott and Allison, and a transfusion of courage, before I went to the principal's office. Now that I'd arranged to meet Joey Dillon, I didn't need to buy tickets. Who wants tickets for a canceled dance!

But Joey found me and gave me two useless tickets free, and talked me into getting a refund for him, and then he tried to sell me a pen. That Joey Dillon is unbelievable.

A group of kids in the hall started stamping their feet and shouting, "Madison School rots!" Soon a crowd gathered and chanted. "Unfair to cancel the dance because a few kids threw snowballs. Unfair."

Suddenly I was shouting too. At first I didn't really shout, I just spoke to myself out loud. "Unfair. Unfair." I was just so angry I didn't realize how loudly I was talking. But then I saw Dana and her friends watching me.

"Someone should speak to Mr. Standish and complain," Dana shouted.

An even louder chant went up as kids shouted, "UN-FAIR! UNFAIR TO KIDS! . . . TELL THE PRINCIPAL! . . . TELL MR. STANDISH WE PROTEST! . . . UNFAIR TO KIDS!"

"You kids better calm down," Mr. Mara, the janitor, yelled as he walked by dragging his dust mop, "or I'll give you UNFAIR all the way to the office at the other end of the building."

A few teachers from nearby rooms tried to quiet us down. One went to ring the intercom for help. Fortunately for us the teacher picked one of the rooms where the intercom never works. Then Dana pulled me up to the front of the crowd.

"Hey, Karen, want a grit before you go to the office? She has to see the principal right now," she added for everyone to hear. "Don't you, Karen?" she asked. "How come you're still here, anyway? It's after seventh period. I heard the secretary. I think Karen should tell Mr. Standish he's unfair."

I was glad Peter was off with his swim team and not here to witness my death by embarrassment. Even some of the other kids looked shocked at the way Dana spoke to me. Scott tried to push through the crowd. I could hear him saying, "Leave her alone." Allison, my best friend, who always knows exactly what to do, was just standing there speechless. Mom, Dad, Beth, Jillie, and Bruno were, of course, out of the picture. I was definitely going to have to do something on my own.

Dana had never been out to get me before. Although she'd never been nice to me, she usually just wanted to be the center of attention. But her next words were like a snowball aimed directly at me on purpose. "You want to go to the dance with Peter, don't you? Well, you better go talk to the principal. You threw the damn snowball at the old man, anyway."

What was she talking about? Okay, maybe she knew Peter had said yes about going with me to the dance. Maybe she'd asked him and he'd said no to her and she was jealous, but what was she talking about—me throwing a snowball at that man? I'd seen all those kids out there throwing snowballs when I was coming into school. Two sixth-graders had started it, but seventh- and eighth-graders had joined in. I'd just thrown one snowball up in the air. I didn't even look to see where it went. I'd been so excited about Peter sprinkling snow on my hair. Who cared about snowballs at a time like that? But it couldn't have—my heart started to beat really fast—it couldn't have been my snowball that hit the old man.

"I heard him myself," Dana's words interrupted my thoughts. "The old guy pointed to the school and said one word—'Karen'—and I said your last name. Mr. Standish heard the whole thing. You got the damn dance canceled, Karen. You get it back!" she said and pushed me toward the doorway.

I felt like I had no bones. I was folding up like a packet of tourist's postcards. But the thought of that hurt old man made me race off to the principal's office. I didn't know what I'd say. And worse yet, what would the principal say to me?

9

Meanwhile,
Back at the Ranch House

The gravel-voiced secretary looked over the top of her glasses and growled, "Name? Name?" she repeated.

"Karen Berman," I said in a whisper. "Mr. Standish wanted to see me?" I hoped Mr. Standish had decided to leave early. No such luck.

"Go right in. He's waiting for you," the secretary ordered.

"Come in, Karen." I heard the principal's voice. I took a deep breath and entered his inner office. Glancing around, I saw a poster on his wall that said, "Children are our future."

"Sit down, Karen. I'm not going to bite you. I just want to hear your side of the story." The principal's chair squeaked as he leaned back.

"Uh, Mr. Standish," I stuttered, "I'm not even sure what the story is about."

"Well, that's a good sign," he said. "I know you've never been in trouble before. That's what's confusing me. You know, of course, that a man named Mr. Alexandrov collapsed here today. And although his being struck by a snowball didn't cause his serious condition, it did contribute to it. He fainted while coming to report the incident."

Well, now I knew the old man's name—Mr. Alexandrov. Poor Mr. Alexandrov.

"Yes, I heard the announcement. But why did you want to see *me?*"

"Did you throw any snowballs today?" Mr. Standish looked right into my eyes and waited patiently for me to answer.

My mouth dried up and I hoped I had a voice. "Just one," I heard myself saying, but felt as if I were someone else watching and listening. One lousy snowball thrown no place, without thinking, and look at the results.

"But I didn't throw it *at* anyone, Mr. Standish. Honest, Something nice had happened and I just tossed one snowball in the air with excitement. That's the truth." I thought of Mr. Alexandrov and the gory lunchroom stories about puddles of blood, bone sticking out, and skin turning blue. I could picture him clutching his heart, and I felt sick. I started to shake and my eyes filled with tears. I wasn't even able to hold the tears back, so they just trickled down my cheeks.

Up until now it seemed like the most awful thing that had ever happened to me was that my hair didn't come out right, or my sister was being rotten to me, or I was worried about Peter and the dance. Somehow all that didn't seem as important now. All I could think of was Mr. Alexandrov.

Mr. Standish didn't interrupt. He listened to what I said and cleared his throat, which made me immediately have to clear mine. I catch all things like that as if they were contagious.

I listened for words like "You're suspended," or "Who do you think you are?" In my mind he'd already spoken. So I was really surprised when he said, "I can see how upset you are. Believe me, you are not alone in this. Several of the other youngsters involved are not new to trouble, and their snowballs were thrown at the man intentionally. But worse yet, they deny their guilt. Their parents have been notified and those students will be disciplined and held responsible. One student even blames you directly."

Dana, of course, I thought.

"Do you know Mr. Alexandrov?" he asked.

"No, I don't know him. But I'd like to."

"He called your name—at least your first name—and according to this other student, *he* was placing the blame on you."

"I don't understand," I said. "I don't know why he called my name. I've seen him walking around the neighborhood, but this morning was the first time I ever spoke to him. And that wasn't at school and had nothing to do with snowballs." I knew I was talking fast. I always do that when I'm upset. But I couldn't stop. "It was near my house that I saw him, when I was feeding the birds this morning," I went on. "He asked my name and I told him and we talked a bit. I didn't even know his name till you said it."

"I see," the principal said, tapping the end of his pen on his desk. "Most of the youngsters involved in this incident were being thoughtless rather than malicious. It seems that when it comes to snowballs, good kids as well as trouble-makers participate. I am sure those youngsters will think twice before tossing snowballs in the future."

"Mr. Standish," I said, trying to keep my voice from quivering, "I just threw this snowball up in the air, not at anyone, honest."

"Where were you standing, Karen?" Mr. Standish asked, "And at what time did you do this?"

I thought for a second, then answered. "I was almost at the school door and I tossed the snowball a little before the bell rang."

"I don't think you meant any harm, Karen, and that's quite different from what several of the other kids intended."

Okay, I knew he believed me, but I still felt upset, just because I supposed I could have hurt the old man. "But what if it was my snowball that hit Mr. Alexandrov? I mean, by accident. Maybe I could visit him in the hospital. My friend's father is a doctor there. Maybe he could get me in to see Mr. Alexandrov."

"Visiting Mr. Alexandrov would be a very nice thing to do," Mr. Standish agreed. "Perhaps you'll be able to help him in some small way. Giving your time to help the man is meaningful and acceptable to me. You may go now, Karen."

"Mr. Standish"—I stood up and tried to feel stronger and more in control, only my knees trembled as I spoke—"one more thing is bothering me. Isn't there something you could do about not canceling the dance? Something that wouldn't punish the innocent kids? You said yourself that most of the kids involved weren't being malicious." I didn't know where I was getting my nerve from, but I felt like I'd struck oil. The more I dug, the more words spouted!

"I understand how you feel, Karen. It is unfair. It was a very difficult decision for me to make. But I have one word that overrides 'unfair' and that's 'unsafe.' I'm afraid the dance is off. It would be too difficult to prevent snowball-throwing in the dark. Can you understand my dilemma?"

"Yes," I answered, and sighed.

I could understand it, and I also felt selfish for even thinking about the dance when Mr. Alexandrov was hurt. But I really didn't think it was fair to punish innocent people.

"I don't see how we could possibly have this dance"—

Mr. Standish thought out loud for a moment, tapping his pen on his desk again. "Although," he said, "we won't have another leap year for four more years. If I remember the *Li'l Abner* cartoon strip correctly, Sadie Hawkins was the character in whose memory a race was run so girls could chase and catch the fellows they liked. It's in honor of leap year too. Also, since I do like the way you're speaking openly to me and caring about justice, I feel it's my duty to respond in some favorable way."

I couldn't believe what I was hearing. I felt ten feet tall. I also was glad to find out who Sadie Hawkins was, anyway.

"How about this?" I suggested, trying to think fast. "So as not to punish the innocent, how about, instead of tomorrow night, having the seventh grade Sadie Hawkins Winter Switch Dance in a month. It's spring weather by the end of March," I went on, "without snowballs." A Winter Switch Dance in spring, I thought, waiting for the principal to answer. Our whole school could join that Procrastinators' Club my dad told me about and celebrate July Fourth in December. I wouldn't even need Joey Dillon to help me sell an idea like that.

"Fair enough," he finally said.

"Thanks," I answered.

"Thank *you*, Karen," he said. "I'll announce the changed dance date and the reasons for it on the public address system in the morning. I think you have the makings of a future leader."

I had the makings of a future leader? I couldn't believe it. I'd handled the whole situation without Mom or Dad, or even Scott or Allison. "Uh, goodbye," I said, and raced out to the girls' room. I felt like a future leader about to be sick. My nerve had dried up.

I was glad the bathroom was empty. I splashed some

water on my face in case my eyes were red. The dismissal buzzer had sounded as I left Mr. Standish's office. I heard the roar of the buses pulling away. I was glad. I didn't want to see any of the kids. I wanted to walk home in the frosty air—to walk like Mr. Alexandrov did and to think about him. I left the school building. As I walked in the snow I wondered if Mr. Alexandrov had any family. And did he think I threw the snowball at him? Deliberately? Maybe he hated me by now.

The snow crunched under my feet and my shoes were good and soggy when I arrived home. I was glad Mom and Dad were both working and had probably lost track of time. I just called hello and went right to my room. I like getting home from middle school before Jillie and Beth get home from grade school. It gives me some time to think. And I had a lot to think about.

Now, when I felt like telling Scott and Allison all about my talk with Mr. Standish, I didn't want to tie up the phone lines, because Peter might call. But there was one phone call I just had to make. At least hospitals don't have unlisted numbers. I phoned hospital Information and was told that Mr. Alexandrov had been admitted but that his condition wasn't listed yet. I left a message to have Scott's father call me. I was glad he was a doctor at Somerset Hospital. I hoped Mr. Alexandrov wasn't real sick or hurt badly. It gave me an empty feeling just thinking about it, as if a snowball had hit me in the stomach.

But then my mind switched back to Peter. Had he tried to get me while the line was busy? Should I call him and say it was Andrew again? Should I tell him the dance had been postponed a month, till the end of March, when it's spring—not canceled? Then maybe he'd ask me to go to a movie tomorrow night instead of to the dance. And should

I explain that I hadn't intended to throw that snowball at anyone? Would Peter still call me? I can ask myself more impossible questions than those on the *$64,000 Question*— a fifties TV quiz show my mom wrote about in her diary.

I picked up Mom's diary from my bed where I'd left it in the morning. I thought about how awful today was and wondered if my mom had had any awful days when she was my age. I looked through the diary pages. The best I could find was:

> April 3, 1955
> *That sister of mine is in for it. She has definitely been reading this diary again. She is so dumb! She left the broken tip of a bobby pin inside the lock and now my key is bent.*
>
> *I wonder how much she read about Mr. X and the day I said I was taking the dog for a walk out front, but instead walked to Mr. X's block and saw him. And he waved, and I waved and said hello. I'm glad I don't ever write his name or she'd never stop teasing me. I was so mad at Judy that I walked into her room and poured a glass of water over her head. How was I supposed to know she was working on this social studies project all week and I ruined it. NOT GUILTY!*

So Mom did know about hairpins opening diaries, and she did at least say hello to Mr. X. And best of all, she did get into trouble once in a while. I couldn't believe my Aunt Judy had been such a pest. If I ever dumped water on Beth's head and project, I'd be punished with no telephone for at least a week. Also, I'd never want my sister Beth to read this and get any ideas from it. I wrote:

MEMO: To myself when I have a teenage daughter. I'll let her know I got into some trouble too when I was her age—and I'll let her know how I got out of it.

The phone rang and I nearly jumped out of my skin. But it wasn't Peter. It was Scott. I summed up the situation in one breath, like a telegram—"Can't talk—Peter may call—school dance postponed till spring—call you later—bye"—and I hung up.

No sooner did the phone hit its cradle than it rang again. I crossed my fingers. That must be Peter. I picked up the phone and heard, "Hello, Karen, it's Allison. What happened with Mr. Standish?"

I repeated the verbal telegram and hung up. Why is it that whenever you're waiting for a special, really important call, everyone else phones? The next call was "Do you want your basement sealed and protected against water damage?" Unlisted number or not, we get calls like that. They must call every number. Usually my dad refers these calls to Jillie, who makes the person crazy. I handled this one myself in one word, "No."

I settled down in my beanbag chair and thumbed through Mom's diary to keep busy while waiting and hoping Peter would call me. I heard Beth and Jillie get home and call hello. I called hello back, adding, "Please don't use the phone. I'm expecting a call." I expected a fight from Beth, but instead Jillie called from the hallway, "Okay, Karen, Beth won't use the phone, because we're eating cookies, and then she promised to listen to me sing 'Farmer in the Dell' right through to the cheese. I have to sing it in school tomorrow. The teacher said. Wanna have cookies with us?"

"Maybe later," I called back. Today I wasn't hungry for a snack and didn't join Beth and Jillie in the kitchen. I was too upset. I wanted Scott's dad to call so I could find out if he could get me into the hospital. I just had to see Mr. Alexandrov, but I also didn't want the phone to be busy. I didn't want to miss Peter's call. How could I think both these things were so important? Mr. Alexandrov being hurt and me talking to Peter. But they did both seem important.

Mom's diary was still open on my lap, and I glanced at a page about club parties, with Spin the Bottle and Post Office kissing games and the new food fad, pizza. When the phone rang, I picked it up.

"Hello," I said.

"Hello. This is Rebecca."

"Rebecca?" I said. "Rebecca who?"

"Uh, Andrew, this is Rebecca—you know who"—and Peter's special laugh tickled me and I burst out laughing too. I curled up in my chair and doodled Peter's name on a nearby pad.

"I'm so glad it's you, Karen," Peter said. "This is the fifth call. I called 6093 and 9063 and 9093 and 6063. I may as well admit it, I'm the mathematics genius who can't read numbers."

"But you got it!" I said.

Now we were both embarrassed. I could hear it in the silence. Then I laughed a silly, nervous "he-he" kind of taking-up-time laugh when you can't think of anything to say. And Peter laughed this special laugh that comes like a wave from deep inside him. I wished I had a laugh like that.

I guess sometimes the best ideas sort of slip out, spur of the moment. Maybe it was Mom's red-leather diary in my lap, open to that page about pizza and club parties. At least

I didn't have to uninvite a boy to the dance, like my mom did. Peter knew it was canceled. After all my worry and work, I didn't want tomorrow night to be a waste either. Maybe I was all warmed up from my talk with the principal. Suddenly I was a Procrastinators' Club dropout. Spring was too far away to be real, and while I was thinking of the dance Peter was telling me how he'd done so well at the swim meet. He probably was too excited to ask about me and Mr. Standish. He also wasn't saying anything about wanting to take me to a movie, as I'd hoped. So I made the big move. Before I knew it the words were out.

"You know," I said, "since there's no dance tomorrow night—"

"They always have stale pretzels anyway," Peter interrupted. "And I get those new dances all mixed up. I think I reverse my feet like I reverse my numbers."

"Can you come to my house tomorrow night instead?" I went on. I figured I'd rather explain everything—about the snowballs, Mr. Alexandrov, and the principal—privately (in other words, without Dana around). "I'm making a—" I stared at the diary, wondering why I'd just said another dumb thing, and added—pizza party." I figured, what kid could refuse pizza? "I'm inviting Scott, and Allison and Jeff, and, oh, Lori," I said, trying to make some sense out of the situation and wondering what was happening to me, planning a party without clearing it with my folks first.

"Sure," Peter said. "A pizza party will be great. What time?"

"Eight o'clock," I said, and I sighed a big sigh of relief until—

"Can I bring—" Peter started to say, when I interrupted him.

"Just bring yourself. I'll take care of all the food. Thanks anyway."

But then he added, "Great. I've got one question, though. Can I bring Dana?"

I couldn't believe what I'd heard. "Can you what?" I said in a shaky voice, hoping I'd heard wrong.

"Bring Dana," he repeated.

I kind of gulped. I was speechless. And the diary fell right out of my hands. Can you love someone one minute and hate them the next? The answer is yes. How could he do that to me?

"Sure," I said, not knowing what else to say.

"See ya," he said. "Bye."

That was that. My future leadership qualities seemed to be like disappearing ink. And as I said goodbye and hung up, I wished Peter Raskin would also disappear. How could he do that to me? Bring a date to my party when he was supposed to be my date! I scratched out his name on my pad. Why couldn't all boys be like Scott, I thought. I threw myself on my bed, making a loud crash as I knocked some books off my night table.

"You okay, Karen?" Mom called from her bedroom across the hall.

And Dad must have thought a bomb fell. That's how it probably sounded downstairs. I soon heard his footsteps.

"What is going on?" Beth yelled. "It's a good thing Jillie's with me. A person could get hurt in your room."

"Karen?" Jillie called, "You okay?"

"No!" I shouted. "I'm not okay! I am suffering from a dread disease called 'foot in mouth.' And with my luck, the foot even has a boot on it!"

I got up from my bed and tried to calm Bruno, who was madly flapping his wings. Then, stepping over the fallen books, I opened the door. My parents, Beth, and Jillie were in the hallway outside my room.

"What crashed?" Dad asked, looking over my shoulder.

"Books," I answered, adding, "Could we have a family meeting in the kitchen in half an hour?" I looked at my watch. "At three-thirty?"

"Can it wait until after dinner?" Dad asked. "I'm working on a difficult experiment. I really can't leave it now."

"That would be better for me too," Mom added. "Dad needs my help for a few minutes, or rather, he needs my hand for the experiment."

"Me three," Jillie said. "I'm not up to the cheese yet in 'Farmer in the Dell.' I'm just up to the child."

"That is the longest song," Beth said, taking Jillie's hand the way I used to take hers. "You're almost finished," she said encouragingly.

"Okay." I said. "We'll have the meeting after dinner." If Scott's dad would only call. Maybe then I could even visit Mr. Alexandrov that afternoon. I just had to see him.

When I was alone again I took out my memo book and wrote.

> MEMO: *To myself when I have a teenage kid.*
> *I will understand if the kid gets into trouble at school or plans a party without asking.*

Even I didn't believe that one.

10

Double Trouble

Just a day before, my life had been so simple, although I hadn't realized it then. Now, like the way the snow suddenly changes the color of the world, my world had changed. What if it had been my snowball that had hit Mr. Alexandrov? And what was I going to do about Dana coming to *my* party? The thought of her made me rip a piece of paper to shreds. And I felt worse because here I was, sitting on my bed worrying about Peter and Dana and parties when maybe Mr. Alexandrov was clinging to life in the hospital. I still couldn't understand how both things could be so important to me at the same time—but they were.

"Come on, call," I muttered as I picked up the books that had fallen and piled them on my desk. I picked up the diary last and curled up in my beanbag chair right next to the phone. I flipped through the pages, wishing there would be a page all about what Mom did at a party. Of course there wasn't. But then I saw a diary entry that made me really curious. I read on.

May 1, 1955

I don't think I should write this. What if someone someday reads this diary? They'll find out too much about me. They'll find out I love Mr. X even though he's much older than me. They may think I'm dumb. Maybe I am, but I can't help it. I think he likes me too. Lately I've seen him walking past my house, and once I saw him look up at it. I actually spoke to him and walked a few blocks with him today. We talked and talked. I wish I could write about it. Then we went to Cooky's restaurant for a soda and he wouldn't let me pay for mine. Is that a date?

I definitely wanted to know more about this diary entry. But at the moment I could only think of Mr. Alexandrov. I decided to call Scott. Maybe he had a faster way of getting in touch with his father.

I almost slipped off the beanbag chair, stretching to reach the phone. I dialed Scott's number. The phone rang and rang. Don't tell me he isn't home, I thought. He finally answered on the tenth ring, huffing and puffing as if he'd just come inside from running.

"Scott, you've got to help me!" I blurted out. "Don't ask a lot of questions, okay? Just give answers like 'yes.'"

"Karen, what are you talking about?" Scott said.

"I've been waiting and waiting for your father to call me back. I left a message for him at the hospital."

"How come you called my father?" Scott asked.

"I need to get to the hospital before afternoon visiting hours are over. I want to visit—or at least find out if the man's all right—the man who collapsed at school. Could you call your father for me? Oh, and listen, because the school dance was postponed, I'm having a pizza party here tomorrow night at eight o'clock. Call Lori and invite her, and would you call Joey Dillon and invite him too? Just him. I need an extra boy."

"Joey Dillon? Since when do you like him? What about Peter?"

"Just say 'yes,' Scott, and come over when it's all arranged. I don't have a minute to spare. I'll explain everything later. Bye."

I hung up the phone and wondered. I didn't know why I was inviting kids to a party I hadn't asked permission to have. It had just happened. If we'd had the family conference at 3:30 the way I'd suggested, I'd probably have permission by now—or maybe I wouldn't. I guess I figured Mom and Dad might not have me cancel a party if I'd already invited a bunch of kids, rather than just Peter. Maybe they'd give in if I promised never to do it again—or would they? I guess I was making my own decisions now, and they weren't all good ones.

The phone rang. I hoped it was Scott's dad calling with news of Mr. Alexandrov, but it was Allison. And before I knew it, I did it again. I blurted out, "Alli, can you and Jeff come to a pizza party at my house tomorrow night at eight o'clock?"

"You're having a girl/boy party? That's really super. Hold on a minute. I'll ask. Maaaaa." I heard her call and yell the question. Then she must have covered the mouthpiece with her hand. I didn't hear anything. I waited, tapping the mouthpiece as if that would get her attention. I didn't want to keep the phone lines busy in case Scott's father was trying to get me. I was getting very worried about Mr. Alexandrov.

"This is stupid," Allison finally said, "but my mother's making me ask it. Are your parents going to be home, and who's invited? My mother asks questions even when she knows the answers. This is one of her 'just in case' questions."

"Sure my parents will be home," I said, and then I felt a moment of panic. They didn't know there was a party yet. They definitely wouldn't allow me to have a party if they weren't going to be home. But what if they'd made other plans, plans they couldn't change? They wouldn't have. I was supposed to be out at the dance, so they would have had to be home with Jillie and Beth anyway. Only what if they'd invited friends over or planned to have a "no nukes" meeting here?

"Who's going to the party?" Allison asked.

When I told her, I got the same reaction as from Scott.

"Joey Dillon? Dana?" Allison muttered. Then she shouted as if her voice had to be heard in the next room, "Her parents will be home." Then she repeated all the names of the kids invited to my party as if her mom had asked her to. I waited, wishing she would hurry.

"Come on, Alli," I muttered, drumming my fingers impatiently on the phone.

Just then Allison was back on the phone. "Uh-oh," she whispered, "my mother wants to think it over. She just asked me if Dana's the girl I once pointed out to her on Main Street. 'The kid who smokes God knows what' is the way my mother put it. My mother's got a memory like an elephant. Is Dana bringing her 'grits,' Karen?" Allison imitated Dana's cool voice. And I started worrying some more. What if she did light up a cigarette? What would I say? Put it out? That would be embarrassing. And what if she did smoke "God knows what" at a party?

"Please, Alli, you've gotta come to the party. I'm scared," I added. "Come right over. I've got a lot to tell you. I can't talk now, I'm expecting a phone call."

"Okay," she said. "I think I can talk my mom into driving me. She has to do some food shopping for a dinner party she's having next week."

"See ya," I said and we hung up.

I reached for my memo book and wrote these lines.

> MEMO: *To myself when I have a teenage kid.*
> *I will love her even if she makes some dumb decisions.*

I guess it was habit that made me glance out the window at 3:15. Not seeing the old man on his scheduled walk made me feel empty.

Scott got to my house a few minutes later and we went to my room. "I'll call my dad before he finishes his rounds at the hospital and leaves," Scott said. "I couldn't reach him before. Maybe he can find out about the guy. I did call Lori and Joey Dillon, though, and they can come to the party."

"I was hoping you'd done that," I said and breathed a sigh. "And if you reach your dad now, could you ask him if I could visit Mr. Alexandrov? That's what I really want to do."

Scott picked up my phone and pushed the number he'd called many times. I guess when your father's a surgeon he's always at the hospital. "Could you page Dr. Fisher, please? This is his son. What did you say the old man's name is, Karen?" Scott asked as he waited for his dad to get to the phone.

"Mr. Al-X-androv." I pronounced the name slowly, thinking to myself, Another Mr. X, and this one's mine.

"Dad?" Scott said.

I didn't hear the rest of the conversation because the doorbell rang. I let Allison in and led her back to my room.

"Jeff and I can come to your party," she announced.

"Great," I said.

"My dad's checking," Scott reported, still on the phone when Allison and I walked into my bedroom. "I explained that you want to visit the man." Scott covered the mouthpiece of the phone as he talked to me.

If he doesn't find him listed anymore, I thought, either it means he was well enough to go home . . . or he died! I couldn't imagine anything that awful. It made me feel too sick. I sank down on the floor, winding pieces of yellow shag carpet around my finger as I waited for Scott to speak. "I'll explain all this in a minute," I said to Allison.

Scott was talking and listening to his father again. Then he finally hung up and repeated Dr. Fisher's words. "Mr. Alexandrov is in fair condition. No apparent broken bones, but he has to stay put for a day or so for observation and tests since he has a previous heart problem. But he can have visitors," Scott went on. "And my dad said he'd sneak you in to see him if you can get a ride over to the hospital right away. Just page him when you get there."

"Great," I said. I could feel my muscles loosen with relief. "Only how am I going to get to the hospital?"

"First, how about explaining to us what is going on?" Scott said, sitting up straighter in my desk chair.

I explained about the one snowball I'd tossed at school. "It could have been my snowball that hit that old man, Mr. Alexandrov. Dana told the principal she heard the man call my name just before he fell."

"You've gotta be kidding," Allison said, curling her feet under her on my bed. "What did you tell the principal? I'd be so scared of what he'd say to me."

That's Allison.

"What did the principal say?" Scott asked. "And what did you say?"

"I told him, since there was even a chance that it could

have been my fault, I felt I had to do something, like visit the guy."

"Did Mr. Standish suspend you?" Allison asked. "I don't know what I'd tell my mother if I was suspended."

"No, he just wants me to see if I can help the man. Maybe the old man doesn't have anything to do," I added, "and that's why he walks all day. I feel awful about tossing that snowball, in case it was mine that hurt him." We were all quiet for a minute, and that's when I heard a slight noise outside my door. When I opened the door, there they were, Beth and Jillie, sitting on the floor in the hall and looking up at me.

"I came to practice singing for you," Jillie said, "and we were just waiting for Scott to get off the phone. Beth said I shouldn't bother Scott and you."

"You threw a snowball at an old man?" Beth said, and Jillie gasped.

But what surprised me most of all was that Beth wasn't talking mean or racing off to blab to Mom and Dad.

"Could you go to jail?" she asked, and she really looked worried, the way she used to look when she was little—not like her usual eleven-year-old looks, hoping I'd go to jail so she could have my room and all my barrettes.

I never thought she cared about me a bit. It made me feel good when she said, "I'll help you, Karen. I won't let anyone take you away. I'll kick them and bend their thumbs back!"

I knew from experience that she was very good at that. Then Jillie grabbed my leg and wrapped her legs around mine, clinging to me like a koala bear until she heard me say, "Thanks, Beth. But don't worry, I'm not going to jail. I'm just going to the hospital."

"Hospital!" Jillie shrieked and raced off, probably to get

Mom and Dad from the basement laboratory. Not telling my parents about the snowball or the party was beginning to be like a dropped ball of yarn, unrolling and getting everyone all tangled up in it. Soon I heard excited voices getting closer and closer. I got up and looked out into the hall. Mom came charging down the hallway, with Jillie attached and Dad behind her.

"What is Jillie talking about, that you're going to the hospital, not to jail? What is going on with you today?" Mom asked, her voice rising with excitement. "Karen, I want to know everything—right now!" Her last words came out in a roar.

I didn't get a chance to say a word, because my father took over. "I am very curious about all this, but right now I can't take time out to know what is happening. I have to finish my project. I am trying to work. W-O-R-K!" He spelled it and stormed off.

"I don't like to yell at you in front of your friends," Mom added, "but you have pushed my patience to the limit."

I took a deep breath and a big chance. I felt terrible upsetting my parents like this, but I just had to do what I had to do. "Can I give your patience one more little shove?" I pleaded. "Take me to the hospital and I'll explain everything in the car."

"Karen, I can't just drop everything to drive you here and there. You're not hurt, are you? Pains in your stomach or anything?" Mom asked.

"No. I'm not hurt or sick. But at school there was a man who was hit by a snowball. And I've got to go see him. I told the principal I would. Please, Mom. You've just got to help me. Pretty please."

"My dad said he'd sneak her in if she hurried down to the hospital," Scott explained, trying to help me.

"Okay, Karen. Only I want an explanation, and it had better be one heck of a story," Mom said. "I don't like this at all. But I'm going to drive you because you made a commitment to go. I have to go out for milk anyway. Beth, get my car keys from the kitchen table. Jillie, get my pocketbook. Karen, get your coat—and *boots*."

Somehow wearing or not wearing boots didn't seem very important anymore. I wasn't about to push my luck. I looked at Allison and Scott, then at Beth and Jillie.

"We can't all go to the hospital," Scott said.

"Scott and I can stay here and plan the party," Allison suggested.

"Sure," I said, "I'll be back soon." I was glad Allison hadn't mentioned "party" while Mom was in the room.

"What party?" I heard Beth say, but I was already on my way down the hall and putting on my jacket.

In the car with Mom I quickly explained about the snowball. I'd wait till the family conference after dinner to break the news about the party. Mom shook her head, muttering, "You've had quite a day. You must have been upset. Imagine the principal thinking you might be responsible, a good kid like you," she said as we drove down Route 206. "One little toss of a snowball and lives are changed."

"But I might be responsible. I don't think I am, but the man did call out my name." I avoided telling her Mr. Alexandrov's name. It was a feeling deep inside me that made me want to keep the name to myself a little longer.

11

At the Hospital
and Home Again

Mom dropped me off at the hospital entrance. She wished me good luck and went on to shop at the Seven-Eleven store nearby. Scott's father answered the page and greeted me, leading the way to the elevator. We rode up to the second floor, then walked down the hall, past the "Caution—floor is wet" sign blocking the way. It smelled like the time I poured too much Clorox bleach into the washer. We stopped at Room 214.

Scott's father gave an "It's okay" kind of wave to a passing nurse who was giving me a mean look. He was going to take me inside, but his pager beeped and he had to answer the call.

"Just visit for five minutes, so you don't tire the man," he instructed me in his doctor voice. "And if anyone gives you a hard time, have me paged."

I entered the room alone, feeling like my legs were numb and my mouth frozen shut—and not from the cold. I looked around. Mr. Alexandrov must have just eaten. They sure serve dinner early in this hospital. It couldn't be later than four-fifteen. The room still smelled of roast chicken and whipped potatoes with gravy. And on his tray table there was a plate piled with the barest chicken bones. I'd never seen bones picked that clean, as if he'd been very hungry.

Mr. Alexandrov peered at me from his bed. He looked like a pale Santa Claus propped up on pillows but wearing a green wool cap, not a red one. Maybe he wears his hat to give him confidence, like I wear striped socks. The little portable radio he holds next to his ear when he walks was right there on his pillow, and when I got up closer I could hear that he didn't listen to waltzes like I imagined he would. Instead he listened to rock music.

There was a person in another bed near the window, but the separating curtain blocked my view. I could just hear him moaning, "Oy, I'm dying." It gave me the shivers.

"Karen," Mr. Alexandrov said, recognizing me. "Come in."

"You're sure I'm not bothering you?" I muttered. "I won't stay long. My mother's picking me up in a few minutes."

"I'm not the kind of person who asks you in one door and shoves you out another," he said, patting his bed for me to come closer.

I sat down in the chair next to his bed. Funny, he didn't yell. He seemed glad to see me.

"Oy, I'm dying," came in a moan from behind the curtain.

"Should I ring for the nurse?" I asked, pointing to the curtain.

"No," Mr. Alexandrov said. "That's Morris, my new friend. He's okay. He just likes to moan. He's only here for gall bladder tests."

Then the voice gave a long moan and said, "Maybe I'm dead?"

"You're not dead, Morris," Mr. Alexandrov said. "You're gonna get better and I'm gonna beat you at gin rummy." Then Mr. Alexandrov looked at me with a sad expression.

"Why do children throw snowballs at an old man?" he asked. With the subject changed to snowballs, I momentarily froze.

"I didn't mean to throw a snowball at you," I finally said, kind of stuttering, and I had to swallow hard to get the words past a lump in my throat.

Then he looked me right in the eyes. "You threw a snowball at me?" he said. "What are you talking about? A nice girl like you? A girl who feeds the birds? No. I don't believe it." He turned off the radio. "Tell me again what you said. I didn't hear right."

"It might have been my snowball. See, Peter, this boy I really like, put snow on my head, and that means he likes me, and I was so happy I threw a snowball in the air and ran inside the school building. I don't know where the snowball went, but maybe it was the one that hit you, and I'm very sorry. That's what I came to tell you."

"I saw you run inside," Mr. Alexandrov said. "I was calling to you, but you didn't hear me call." Then Mr. Alexandrov pointed to the closet. "Open that closet," he said, and I got up, walked to the closet, and opened the door. "See my jacket hanging on the hook? Look in the jacket pocket and bring me the paper that's there." I followed his orders. "I'm sorry the paper is crumpled up, but I was hurt already, so I just pushed it into my pocket."

I had no idea what he was talking about, but I did find the crumpled paper. I returned to the chair by his bed and sat down.

"Uncrumple it," he said. "Read."

I smoothed out the paper and saw my own handwriting

and my name and English class on top. It was my English homework. We'd had to write a letter to someone we miss. I'd written to my grandfather in Florida. We were supposed to write a letter that would make the person feel emotion. I'd worked really hard on that assignment. I didn't think it was good, though. It sounded gushy to me. I'd written:

> Dear Grandpa,
>   My pillow is wet with my tears.
> I cry every night because I won't see
> you for so long. Why did you have to
> move so far away?

And on and on. I'd never send a letter like that to my own grandfather. Sure, I miss my grandparents in Florida, but we talk a lot on the phone, and we visit them once in winter and they visit us in the summer. I know they feel better in warm weather. This letter was for my English teacher—to make *him* cry.

As I read it I saw Mr. Alexandrov staring at me, and his eyes looked teary.

"I knew you'd want that letter. I found it in the snow. You must have dropped it when you were feeding the birds or at the bus stop. I couldn't help reading it. I walked to the school, and I saw you. Then, smack—snowballs were flying. I called your name and started to chase the snowball-throwers, and next thing I know, splat—I was on the ground. Rotten kids. Why do they want to hurt an old man? It wasn't you, Karen. You had your back to me and were almost inside by then."

I breathed a sigh of relief. It hadn't been my snowball.

"No, it was a girl with a cigarette package sticking out of

her pocket, and some other boys and girls too!" Mr. Alexandrov added.

It might have been Dana or Gwen or a few others I could think of, but it wasn't me, and I was glad.

"Oy, I'm dying," Morris in the next bed moaned.

"You're not dying, Morris," Mr. Alexandrov answered. "Stop eating rich food and walk a lot like me and I'll dance at your birthday when you're one hundred."

A nurse peeked in. "You'd better go now," she said to me. "You've had more than five minutes."

"Oh, let her stay," Mr. Alexandrov said.

"I better go," I said, not wanting to make him tired, even though I wanted to know more about his walking and staring at my house. "Anyway, I don't want to keep my mother waiting," I added. "Is there anything I can do for you?"

"Nice girl," he said and patted my hand. "Yes, two things. One—if you could walk for me tomorrow. I'll write out where you should stop and what you should say or do. There will be some who won't understand if I'm not there, okay? Get me a paper and pencil from the drawer." He pointed to the table next to his bed. I gave him the paper and pencil and he wrote.

"Oy, I'm dying," Morris moaned.

"You're not dying, Morris," I said. "Mr. Alexandrov said you're going to feel better and play gin rummy."

"Nice girl, Karen," Mr. Alexandrov said. "And call me Charlie. All my friends do."

Finally he handed me the paper. It was a map of my neighborhood with instructions on it. I didn't read it then. My time was up. "I will see you when I'm walking again," Mr. Alexandrov said. "And, oh yes—the second thing you can do for me. When you are so sad and miss your grandpa,

like in that letter, come walk with me, because my grand-
children are far away too. When my wife died five years
ago I moved out of this town and lived with my daughter.
But this year I'm back, ready to make a new life for myself."

He patted my hand again and I patted his hand. "Nice
man, Mr. Alexandrov—Charlie," I said. "You'll be better,
and I'll beat you and Morris at gin rummy. And next time
you walk by my house, stop in and say hello. Okay?"

"Okay," he said.

"Promise?"

"I promise," he answered. "The very next time I pass
your house, I'll stop in and say hello to you. A promise is a
promise." He seemed happy at that idea.

As I got up I put the two papers in my pocket. Maybe
Mr. Alexandrov needed to think I was sad. Maybe it would
help him to get better, I thought.

Then he said something I couldn't figure out. As I waved
from the doorway, he said, "And Karen, say hello to your
mother for me." That's when I got this crazy idea. Was my
Mr. X Mom's Mr. X too?

As I walked out of the hospital room, my imagination
started working. Why had Mr. Alexandrov said, "Say hello
to your mother for me?" He didn't even know my mother.
Or did he? He did have an X in his name. Even I had
thought of calling him my Mr. X.

But he couldn't really be the Mr. X from Mom's diary.

Nah! That's ridiculous, I thought. Sure, the diary said
Mom loved an older guy, but even I couldn't imagine he'd
be that much older than she was—old enough to be Mr.
Alexandrov. But if he was Mr. X, maybe that explained
why he looked at my house every day. Maybe I look the
way my mom looked when she was my age.

As I walked slowly down the hall to the elevator and saw
Mom waiting for me outside the hospital entrance, I

decided the time had come. I'd ask my mother about Mr. X. But when I reached her side, I figured maybe I'd just wait to ask until after my party—just in case I shouldn't have asked at all.

Mom was glad to hear the man was doing well and that he'd said it wasn't my snowball that had hit him.

"What's his name?" she asked. "Do I know him?"

I was wondering if she knew him too. "He told me to call him Charlie. He's a friendly old man. He says hello to everyone," I said, sort of giving her his message and staring at her to see if the first name, Charlie, meant anything to her. Explaining how I really wanted to handle this situation myself gave me a way to avoid mentioning Mr. Alexandrov's last name. In case he was Mr. X, I didn't want to start any trouble. It also avoided having to explain about the map and instructions I was holding. I would have asked Mom more questions but her mood changed.

She clicked her tongue, then said, "Darn. I forgot to get the ice cream while I was at the store. What good is apple pie without ice cream?"

Or did she change the subject on purpose?

I glanced at the map and instructions Mr. Alexandrov had given me. "Oh! I need something from the store too. Can we stop off? You need ice cream anyway. I could just run in and get it for you."

"Good idea," Mom said.

It was getting dark as we headed for the Seven-Eleven store. I figured Scott and Allison had probably left my house already. I was anxious to get home too. Now that I knew Mr. Alexandrov—Charlie—was okay, what I really wanted to do was get back to the diary and see what else I could find out about Mr. X—any clues to see if he could possibly be Mr. Alexandrov.

I also had to concentrate on Peter and the party and what

to do about Dana. Time was running out. It made me mad just thinking of Peter inviting Dana to my party. Dummy—why did I say "Sure, it's okay"? I wanted it to be a really good party, not my biggest embarrassing moment. I also had the family conference to face after dinner and I still had to get permission to even have the party.

Mom pulled into the Seven-Eleven store parking area, and I got out of the car. "I'll just be a second," I said, but she decided to come with me, anyway. I looked around the store for what I needed, sniffing coffee and cold-cut smells. My stomach started to grumble. I wished Mom would hurry, but she kept remembering other things we needed—like toilet paper and laundry detergent—things she'd forgotten to buy when she'd been here just a few minutes before. She'd probably been writing an article in her mind at the same time she shopped. I raced here and there, helping her.

While Mom waited at the checkout counter, I took the papers out of my pocket again, looked at the map and instructions Mr. Alexandrov had given me, and searched around the store for what I needed. I found the pet food section, and took a small box of dog biscuits from the shelf. "I need these too," I said to Mom, and put the box on the checkout counter.

"Karen, we don't have a dog," she said.

"I know. I just need them," I said. "I'll pay you back. It's to help the old man tomorrow."

"Dog biscuits?" she asked, tilting her head and raising her eyebrows.

"Trust me," I said. "It's a long story."

We got home almost at dinner time. Scott and Allison had gone home already. I'd have to phone them later to discuss party plans and to bring them up to date on Mr.

Alexandrov, I thought as I put away the groceries.

Dad and Beth had dinner ready for us. Jillie had set the table. I could tell because the forks were on the right instead of on the left sides of the plates.

At dinner Dad said, "Karen, you are walking on thin ice. If I were you, I would not sit at the table today cracking my knuckles and slurping my soup!"

"But, Dad—" I started to say, then stopped.

My dad has this thing with noises at meals. He can't stand "foods that talk back to him," or kids who talk back. At breakfast he never eats cereals that snap, crackle, or pop.

"What I want to hear about right now is every last detail of this snowball-principal-hospital incident," he said.

So I went through it all again between mouthfuls of the vegetable, beef, and noodle soup Dad had heated up for dinner. Since explaining how I really wanted to handle this myself had worked so well on Mom, giving me a way to avoid mentioning Mr. Alexandrov's name, in case he was Mr. X, I gave the same explanation to Dad. I didn't want to start any trouble between my mother and father. I was surprised that Dad didn't insist on knowing the old man's complete name. Just "Charlie" seemed to satisfy everyone.

After he'd finished his lecture No. 3 on responsibility and carelessness, he and Mom exchanged glances. Then he switched the subject to some exciting news of his own. "The bionic hand is working great, really great. In fact," Dad said, "I think it's finished. All that's left to do is write up my report."

"Honey, that's wonderful." Mom leaned over and kissed Dad right on the lips, and he kissed her back. I wondered if she'd ever kissed Mr. X like that. Beth stared at them and Jillie giggled.

"Now, if nothing goes wrong, I'll be able to bring the finished bionic hand to Washington early next week."

"What could go wrong?" Beth asked.

"Nothing will go wrong," I said. "Daddy's worked so hard on this for years already. Let's give him a hand—ha-ha." We laughed and clapped at what might be our last family hand joke.

"Nothing will go wrong, Daddy," Jillie said. "I won't even go near the speriment. I promise."

"What will you work on next?" I asked.

"I think I'll work on a bionic mouth, " Dad said, joking. "I'll use you, Jillie, and Beth as models."

"Oh, Daddy," Jillie said and giggled again.

"Now on to the important questions, like what's for dessert?" Dad asked.

"Karen selected dessert," Mom announced, and I couldn't imagine what she meant. "It's dog biscuits. Apparently it's her new favorite. Just joking," she added, winking at me while the others gave her odd looks.

"I'm helping the old man by walking his morning route and following his instructions and marks on the street map he drew for me," I said. "And the dog biscuits are part of the first stop. It's okay. Trust me."

"I don't want you walking around the neighborhood very early in the morning by yourself," Dad said.

"This isn't the city, you know," I said. "What's out there—an attack bunny rabbit? It's safe."

Jillie and Beth both giggled.

"It's deserted. The city is safer in the morning. People walking to work. Here it's wilderness," Dad said. "Take someone with you or don't go." He was using a voice that said "I mean it!"

I'd thought about taking Beth with me, but I didn't

mention it yet. I just pleaded, "Ma," but she shrugged her shoulders, then served the apple pie with ice cream on top.

I went to my room and slammed the door. I took out my memo book and scribbled angrily:

> *MEMO: To myself when I have a teenage kid.*
> *I will let my kid slurp soup. I will even teach her how.*
> *And I will let her walk places alone, even at night.*

I put my memo book away and took Mom's diary from my desk. I curled up in my beanbag chair and searched through the diary. I didn't find any more pages about Mr. X, just those couple of places where it looked like pages had been ripped out. I wondered if Mom still had the missing pages. When had she torn them out—years ago or just before giving the diary to me? Most of all I wondered what they had written on them. I went back to May 9, 1955, the Mr. X entry where Mom had written, "Lately I've seen him walking past my house, and once I saw him look up at it."

Just a coincidence, I figured. In the city lots of people walk by and look up at other people's houses. Mr. X couldn't be Mr. Alexandrov. I closed the diary and put it away. I would definitely have to ask Mom about Mr. X— any day now. But first I had to deal with the scheduled family conference and break the news about my party.

12

The Fabulous Fifties
. . . Yawn

I'm glad we have this family policy. Anyone can call a meeting if there's something important to discuss. And since I'd called this one, and it was scheduled for after dinner, I figured I'd better go to it and not sulk in my room.

Jillie had called the last meeting. It had only been about getting better cookies and snacks in the house, but we counted it anyway. Beth had called the one before that to complain about how I get to stay up later than she does. And if I remember correctly, Mom called the one before that to demonstrate to us, as she called it, "The complex art of putting a new roll of toilet paper in the holder, since, regardless of the amount of schooling and intelligence, apparently no one but I seems able to do it." Or was it Dad—who'd had a screaming fit about how no one turned off the shower all the way, and it dripped so much it leaked into his lab?

I also wanted to ask about May 9, 1955. My mom in love with an older man? At my age she was deciding about an older man and dates. I'm having trouble deciding about a boy/girl party.

I walked through the family room and into the kitchen, as ready as I'd ever be for the family conference. Everyone was just finishing dessert, and I was kind of sorry I'd stormed off and missed having some. We all cleaned up the kitchen. Then I sat down in my seat at the kitchen table.

"Family conference, remember?" I said.

"That's right," Dad said, and sat down. Mom, Jill, and Beth did the same.

"So what's up?" Mom asked.

"You know how you're always saying we're all in this family together, and we're supposed to try to understand each other and work out problems together? Well, I sure hope you're ready to understand me."

"I thought you'd already told us all about the trouble with the snowball. There's more? Well, go ahead, shoot," Dad said, and Jillie pretended to shoot with her fingers.

"Shoot me is what you may do when you hear what I've done."

"We're listening," Mom said.

"I seem to have made some big decisions all by myself."

"Nothing wrong with that," Dad said.

"We encourage you to do that," Mom agreed.

"What's a decision?" Jillie asked.

"When your mind tells you what to do," I explained. "And my mind seems to have made a party," I went on.

"Now can I tell about it?" Beth said. "Scott and Allison made me promise not to say a word till you said it was okay."

"Where and when is this party?" Dad asked.

"Uh, here—tomorrow night, Thursday, at eight o'clock. There's no school the next day because of teachers' workshops. That's why the dance was scheduled for that night. And the cancellation of the dance was such a disappointment to me and my friends that I figured a party would be the only thing that would cheer us up. And I seem to have invited boys and girls," I added. "Four of each to be exact, including me. And pizza was also mentioned."

I didn't even have to look up to know that Mom and Dad were looking at each other. I could feel it. I usually only get that feeling when certain teachers stare at me because I'm not paying attention.

"You planned a party without asking us first?" Mom said.

Dad's mouth was silent, but his expression was loud and clear.

"Well, I didn't exactly plan it. It just seemed to happen when I was talking to Peter. Then I invited some other kids—kind of on purpose, I guess," I admitted. "Do you have plans for tomorrow night?" I asked, dreading the answer.

"As a matter of fact," Dad said, "we were supposed to go to the movies with Scott's parents, and you were supposed to baby-sit for Jillie and Beth. But we'd already changed those plans because you had the dance to go to."

"Now that I'm eleven, can't I baby-sit?" Beth interrupted.

"In another year, Beth," Dad said.

"I'm not a baby!" Jillie protested.

"I don't understand why you couldn't just ask permission first, Karen," Mom said.

"Is that asking too much of you?" Dad looked angry. I could see the vein on the side of his forehead start to beat as he spoke. "I don't like to feel that you've taken us for granted."

"But, actually, you kind of took me for granted too," I said. "You wouldn't have had to change your movie plans if, in the first place, you'd asked me if I had plans, or if I wanted to baby-sit." I knew I had them there, and I relaxed. My parents always stressed logic. For once it was on my side.

"True," Mom said. "We just figured you'd be home to do it, until you told us about the dance. I didn't expect a dance to be on Thursday night."

"I have to admit, you do have a point there, Karen," Dad said.

"She does," Beth added, to my surprise.

"Yeah," Jillie echoed.

Mom and Dad exchanged glances and eye signals.

"Since we already had changed our plans and will be home," Dad said, "you can have your party this time."

"Not because you already invited people," Mom added. "I don't like that at all. But because we want you to make your own decisions, and I for one, after reading my diary, was reminded of some unwise decisions I made at your age."

"But in the future we're to be asked first," Dad said. "Do you understand?"

"Yes," I said. "Thanks, you guys."

"And," Mom added, "I assume that you will come up with the allowance money to pay for the pizza?"

"And the cleanup will be your responsibility too," Dad said.

"Do we know the boys and girls you invited?" Mom asked.

"You know Scott, Allison, Lori, and Jeff, and you said you knew Peter Raskin's mother, although you don't know him. You just have never met Joey Dillon or Dana."

"I'm sure if they're your friends that they're well behaved," my dad said with such confidence.

I hoped he was right. I wasn't so sure about Dana.

"Do you agree about the cleanup and cost responsibility?" Mom asked.

"Agreed, but I'm broke."

"Can I go to your party?" Jillie asked. And her eyes sparkled. "I'm not broke."

Jillie is one of those kids who has all the pennies anyone ever gave her because she smiles her cute smile and everyone, including me, buys everything for her.

"That's sweet of you, baby," Dad said. "Oops, I mean Jillie," he said, correcting himself.

"It's not sweet," Jillie said. "I didn't say I'd give her my money. I just said I'm not broke."

Dad reached over and messed up Jillie's hair.

"We'll have our own party—you, Daddy, Beth and me," Mom explained. "Karen's growing up and needs her own space."

"This time she does need real space," Dad added. "Karen, you can use the kitchen and the front room of the basement—just don't let anyone near the back and my lab. Not for any reason."

"And we'll let everyone know we're here, but then we'll stay out of your way," Mom said. "That's my rule. What do you think—fair or unfair?"

"Fair," we all agreed, and suddenly some of my problems, even what to do about Dana, sounded less impossible. Still serious but not impossible.

I didn't mention that Dana was always in trouble, or might have cigarettes with her, or that Peter was bringing her. I still wanted to handle some more things myself.

"What did you do at a party in the fifties, when you were my age? I didn't find much about that in your diary." At least that got it to the subject I wanted. The diary. (And what did you do about loving an older man? I wanted to ask Mom, but didn't. The diary said she didn't want anyone to know. And now I wondered if I should ask about it at all.)

"The diary gives me an idea," Mom said. "Why don't you make your party a fifties party? Kids could dress up like in the movie *Grease* or like The Fonz in *Happy Days* on TV. In my diary I've got lots of stuff describing clothes. Karen, run and get the diary for details," Mom added. And Dad went to get his memory box, remembering that yesterday, in the basement, he'd promised to show that box of treasures to me. I was really interested in the fifties, but did I have to see all this now?

Dad must have known exactly where his memory box was because he was back in the kitchen before me, placing the cigar box on the table.

I handed Mom the diary. "Just remember this is not a birthday party like I used to have when I was little." I wished I hadn't said that. It brought back more memories. I wished my parents, like my stereo, could just be turned off with the touch of a button or a pull of a plug. Nothing could stop them now.

"Remember, your sixth birthday was a sprinkler party and everyone came in bathing suits," Mom said. "Only it turned out there was a solar eclipse and we all had to go inside so we wouldn't look up at the sun." Mom and Dad laughed at the memory.

"Oh, Karen," Mom said, "wasn't the school dance supposed to have been a Sadie Hawkins Day Dance? That's from the fifties too. Maybe we could decorate the basement to look like the town Dogpatch, from the comic strip *Li'l Abner*, and people could dress like Mammy Yokum and Daisy Mae. The girls asked the boys, right?"

"Right," I said.

"So you could have a Sadie Hawkins Day Party," Mom suggested.

"These days every day is Sadie Hawkins Day," Dad

added. Beth and I exchanged looks.

"Forget it, Ma," I said. "I really don't think it would go over very big."

Then Dad opened the cigar box and took out some treasured, old, dusty, class pictures and some old wallet-sized photos. I have to admit I got caught up in the fun.

I loved this one picture of Mom as a young teenager wearing a double pair of socks. I wondered if two pairs of socks made you more confident than one pair of striped socks. In the photo, Mom had on a sweater and scarf, a long plaid skirt, and she wore her hair in a ponytail. She didn't look like my mom at all. But what was really weird was that she wore a red dog collar around her ankle. That really cracked Jillie up.

"A fad," Mom explained. "If the dog collar was on one leg it meant you were available, and if it was on the other leg it meant you were going steady. Only I don't remember which leg meant what."

Then I thought of the secret in Mom's diary. I wondered if she ever went out with Mr. X on a real date, not just a soda, and if she ever told Dad about May 9, 1955. But what if she hadn't told him? I couldn't ask now. I tried to get the conversation back to the party.

"I can't telephone them all again and tell them to dress up in fifties clothes," I said. "Anyway, I've had enough of the telephone for a while. And besides, they might laugh at the idea. Dressing up is babyish."

"Quick! Write that down. Karen is tired of the telephone. This is a historic moment," Dad said.

But it didn't work. Mom was still in the fifties. I had to force myself to listen even a little bit. I felt like I'd snore any minute—and I don't even snore.

Then Mom dragged out a dusty carton of old records for me to use at my party. "We used to rate records like 'That's a ten. I like it. You can dance to it,' " she explained.

"Your mom saves everything," Dad said.

I looked through the records with her just to be polite. After all, she was letting me have the party.

I yawned. No one got the hint. I wished parents were on a timer. You could ask a question and set the timer for a one-minute answer, instead of a lecture and fifteen minutes of "show and tell."

Finally I decided to take charge of this conversation again and spoke up. "Can I change the subject back to my party? My pizza party? Not the fifties," I said.

Mom and Dad looked up. Dad reached over and patted Mom's hand. "We really got carried away, didn't we?" Dad said. After showing us just one more thing, this radio detective Sam Spade badge No. 137596, he closed his cigar box.

"Let's hear about your party, Karen," Mom said.

"Do kids still play Pony Express?" Dad asked.

"What's 'Pony Express'?" I fell for Dad's line, but good.

"Post Office, but with a little more horsing around," he said. "Like this." He got up, grabbed Mom, and hugged and kissed her.

I love when Mom and Dad fool around like that. "Is Pony Express a fifties joke?" I asked.

"Yeah," he said, smiling. "So tell me—what do you do at parties in the eighties?"

"What do we do at our parties? An excellent question," I said. "I have to call Scott and Allison and discuss party plans. Thanks for your ideas, even if I don't use them. But I sure could use your help with the pizza."

"I'll help eat it," Jill announced. She and Beth were busily examining the collection of objects in Dad's memory box.

"Could one of you pick up the pizza and deduct the cost

from my next few months' allowance?" I asked.

"Tell you what," Beth said. "I'll pay for half if you let me come to your party."

"No way," I said. "This is for big kids only."

"This is Karen's party, Beth," Mom added, and Dad agreed.

I wished my party would be like a pizza pie, just fit together so nicely in eight even slices. No such luck, not with Dana coming tomorrow night. She was like an extra piece that didn't fit.

"You better come up with party ideas or else you all might end up eating pizza and staring at each other," Mom said.

I found myself staring at her, knowing that at my age she'd had to think about loving an older man. And here I felt so worried about a dumb party.

What if having only eight kids was too small a party to be any fun? What if I ended up with Joey Dillon, and Dana and Peter stayed with each other? Tomorrow would be *the* big night. My first boy/girl party—my own decision and possibly my own disaster.

Mom and Dad went back to work before I could get Mom alone to ask her any more about Mr. X. I went to my room and called Allison. I also called Scott. Neither she nor Scott had come up with any good party ideas this afternoon.

Then I made quick work of my homework and headed for the shower. I wanted to get to bed early so I'd be up in time to walk Mr. Alexandrov's route before school. At least now I knew my house was his last morning stop. The next morning I'd know lots more. I'd give in and let Beth go with me so I wouldn't be "alone in the wilderness" and so I'd still be allowed to have my party tomorrow night. Of course the bathroom door was closed. Beth always gets there first. I took a deep breath and got ready for our usual fight to get Beth to hurry out of the shower.

But when I shouted, "Beth. Hurry up already," she answered, "Sure, Karen. I'll be right out." And she was.

My mouth hung open as she breezed by me. Something was up. She probably was being extra nice so I'd invite her to my party. Whatever the reason, it sure felt good not to fight—for a change. But when I went to get into bed, it wasn't empty. Beth was in it.

"I gotta talk to you," she said. "Jillie's asleep in our room so I waited for you in your bed."

Then she surprised me with her question. "Who's Mr. X, Karen?"

I was speechless. So she went on. "While you were at the hospital, after Scott and Allison left, and Jillie went down to pester Daddy, I was looking at your nail polishes when I saw that red diary. It was open on your desk. I couldn't help peeking. Then I started to read about Mr. X and about Aunt Judy, and I saw it said 1955, that it was Mom's diary, not yours. What's this with Mom and Mr. X?"

Part of me wanted to murder Beth for being in my room, for even looking at my nail polish without asking, and certainly for looking in the diary—especially if she thought it was mine! Since she's reached eleven, she's been getting me crazy. But I also really needed to talk to someone about all the things I've been thinking. I mean about Mom and Mr. X and Mr. Alexandrov. And for once it seemed more important to talk than to fight. I figured maybe if I needed Beth to be nice and act like a friendly sister, and I let her know that—well, maybe she would.

I sat down next to her on my bed and told her what I'd been thinking about Mr. X, and said I'd really like her to walk Mr. Alexandrov's route with me. She looked up at me and smiled. It made me feel good. Only I still didn't want her sneaking around my room in the future. So I added, "But if you *ever* go through my things again, I will never speak to you again."

I guess maybe she liked my talking to her, because she said, "I won't. I promise." She got up.

"But you're still not coming to my party. It's really just for older kids. Okay? Now, good night," I said. Then I called after her, "I'll meet you in the kitchen, dressed and ready, at six-thirty in the morning. First stop, dog biscuit delivery."

"Okay," she answered, and I hoped that meant she wouldn't be a pest at my party as well. But then again, that would be like expecting miracles.

13

Mr. X Marks the Spot

In the morning Beth and I bundled up and stuffed some bread into our pockets. Jillie was still in bed when I told her I'd take her with me that afternoon to shop for party snacks, and she could have some. She was still sleepy so she only fussed a little about not coming with us then.

I left a note for Mom and Dad, although they'd probably oversleep without any bathroom fight noise to wake them up. Beth and I decided to have breakfast when we got back. I grabbed the box of dog biscuits and we were on our way—boots, scarves, mittens, and all. We walked out into the snow like in *Dr. Zhivago*, a movie I'd seen on TV.

Just the two of us, tracking in the snow like this, all bundled up, reminded me of when we were little kids. We didn't fight as much then. We played all kinds of games, like being rescue-squad people saving lives and being bike racers on our three-wheelers. Beth and I always had very good imaginations. Maybe that's why we were so filled with this Mr. X stuff.

The first spot Mr. Alexandrov had marked on the map was five blocks up and two blocks over. Beth and I talked a mile a minute while we walked.

"If Mr. Alexandrov *is* Mom's Mr. X, do you think Mom would recognize him? I mean, now that he's so old-looking?" I asked Beth as we walked the route drawn on the map.

"I don't know," Beth answered. "Do you think she might *still* love him?"

"I don't know," I answered.

We both got quiet for a minute, and when I looked at Beth I saw she had this worried look on her face. I figured I was making her nervous.

"Look at that snowman over there," I said, pointing to this sorry-looking imitation of a snowman in a front yard across the street. Then I changed the subject to our own memories.

We talked about the snowman we'd once built and how we wanted to put a gravestone where it had melted. We talked about the time we were sick during the first snow of the year. We were little and miserable. Dad and Mom surprised us and brought in snow and put it in the freezer for us to play with when we got better. Before we knew it, we'd walked and talked our way to the first stop. It was a two-story house, much older than ours. We must have been right on time, because this big collie came charging out and started sniffing at our pockets.

I'd forgotten to open the box of dog biscuits under my arm. I took off my mittens, struggling to hold onto the box and not get knocked over by the collie.

"Hold these," I said to Beth, and she took the mittens. "Nice doggie," I murmured as the collie growled. "Nice doggie. Big doggie," I said to the dog, which was now jumping at me as I struggled to open the box of dog biscuits.

"Nice doggie," Beth repeated, petting him.

I fed the dog about three of the biscuits. "From Mr. Alexandrov," I said, as if the collie could understand. The dog licked his chops and raced back up to the front porch and munched the last biscuit.

"Whew!" Beth said. "I thought he was going to knock us over."

"He almost did," I said, laughing. "That was one excited dog. I bet he'd be upset if no one came to give him his morning biscuits and pat on the head. That's what Mr. Alexandrov had been worried about."

As we were taking a last look at the dog on the front porch, Beth said, "Isn't this a pretty house? Look, it has the same stair railing as on our front porch."

"It almost looks like a two-story older version of our house," I said. It really did.

We walked on to the next spot marked on the route. It was two blocks farther on the right. The instructions said: "Feed birds. Fill feeder hanging from cedar tree in front yard."

Beth found the feeder, and we took the squished bread from our pockets, tore it up, and put the pieces in the wooden feeder shaped like an open-sided house. We looked to see if there were any birds around. In a minute or two a bird flew over. Then more and still more gathered to nibble at the bread scraps. Tiny sparrows and squawking blue jays. "From Mr. Alexandrov," Beth shouted, imitating me.

We laughed. This was fun.

Our next stop was on the way back, across the street. It was a one-story house but bigger than ours. It had the same stair railings too. Come to think of it, so did the last house, where we'd fed the birds. I looked at the other houses nearby. None of them even had front porches. Beth and I looked at the instruction sheet. All it said was to watch the last window on the left and wave. "What time is it?" I asked Beth.

She checked. "Six fifty-five." We were right on time.

We both looked at the window and waved. It was such a cute sight to see this baby in bright yellow pajamas waving back from its crib next to the window. It was giggling too and drooling a toothless grin. We waved again.

"I think Mr. Alexandrov is a very nice person," I said.

"Me too," Beth agreed.

"He cares about dogs and birds and babies," I added.

We had one more stop to make before going back home. This was a small house, but it had that same stair railing. Here, as the instructions said, we took the newspaper from its delivery box and brought it to the door. An older woman in a housecoat opened the door and quickly took it in. "Thank you, Mr. Alexandrov," she called into the cold breeze before quickly closing her door. She never looked to see who was there.

Next stop on the map was our own house. And the instructions said, "Just look at the front windows and think of me." So that's what we did. We thought about Mr. Alexandrov and wondered what this was all about. Beth and I looked at each other and shrugged our shoulders. Then we went inside and made hot chocolate and warm buttered toast for us and Jillie. Just as I thought, Mom and Dad were still asleep. I dashed off to the bus stop. Beth's grade school bus wouldn't leave for another half hour, and Jillie goes to afternoon kindergarten, so Mom and Dad would soon be up and Beth would tell them about our walk.

The warm feeling I had from Mr. Alexandrov's route and the hot chocolate and Beth being nice didn't last long.

When I got to the bus stop I saw Peter and Dana walking together, and I felt steaming mad that Peter had asked Dana to my party. At first, when I saw them walking together, I didn't know what to say or do. But when Peter got to where I was standing, near the stop sign, he winked at me, a really special wink like saying something. And I automatically winked back, just as I automatically cough if someone coughs. I didn't think about it, I just did it, and much to my surprise I didn't die of embarrassment.

Then Peter threw a snowball at me. I didn't have time to think much about Dana, because kids kept asking whether I'd spoken to the principal. I had to explain that the dance *would* be held, but in about a month, at the end of March, when it wasn't likely that there could be a snowball fight, since it rarely snows in spring. Kids patted my back and said, "Nice going." But what really put me in a good mood was the white snow spot I knew was on the back of my jacket, made by that gently tossed snowball thrown by none other than Peter Raskin! That two-timer!

Scott pointed to the spot and whispered to me as we were getting on the bus, "Peter does like you, so what's with Dana?"

"That's what I can't figure out either."

We were only in homeroom a minute or so when the principal himself announced over the loud speaker that the dance was postponed instead of canceled. More kids made a fuss over me, saying, "Congratulations."

Allison and I stopped speaking out loud about my pizza party after homeroom, because Tina, the girl who sits in front of me, and Ron the boy next to her, asked if they could come. Even back in fourth grade, Ron never waited to be picked for relay races. He always said, "Could I be on your team?" I figured I'd have to sit next to these kids for

the rest of the year, so how could I say no? I didn't. I said
yes. Now I'd have to tell my parents I'd invited two more
kids without asking first.

But for the rest of the day all talk about the party was
done by passing notes. I didn't want other kids to try to
invite themselves to it, or feel bad about not being invited.
I was glad Joey Dillon wasn't selling tickets to my house.
You never know with him, the way he makes a business out
of everything.

The morning seemed to drag. I don't understand how
the same number of hours can go so fast at home and so
slowly at school. I must have a clock in my brain. I always
get bored ten minutes before the period ends. Instead of
doodling hearts and arrows like I usually do, today I made
lists of things to do for the party, like shopping for soda and
popcorn, and so on.

In Social Studies, Allison and I passed notes about what
to wear and what not to wear tonight, back and forth, until
Mrs. H, the teacher with the hard-to-pronounce name,
said, "Note-passing is not allowed in school," and she
ripped one up.

I couldn't believe it when Dana not only sat next to me
but when she stuck up for me. I felt a little suspicious as to
why.

"That's private property, Mrs. H," she said. "You're not
supposed to destroy it."

"And you're not supposed to talk back, young lady,"
Mrs. H reminded her.

I was surprised at the way Dana was trying to be nice to
me. I couldn't figure her out. I wondered if it was because
she'd been invited to my house for the party or if she was
setting me up for something. I had no reason to trust her.

"What about freedom of speech?" Dana added, sounding

fresh. But at least she didn't storm out of the room or drop her books and cause a commotion, like she usually does. She just waited till Mrs. H was writing on the board and then she whispered to me, "I think Mrs. H would have been much happier if instead of being a teacher, she worked in a mortuary, where no one talks back!"

I couldn't help laughing, kind of covering my mouth so Mrs. H wouldn't have an attack. But I didn't laugh long. When I thought about tonight, with Dana at my party, I hoped I wouldn't end up crying.

The afternoon dragged on even worse than the morning. I started to get excited and scared feelings about the party. And in gym we had to use those wrestling mats that smell like dead fish, which meant I'd have to wash my hair again unless I wanted to smell like a dead fish for my first boy/girl party. And, anyway, gymnastics makes my hair greasy for some reason.

But after school, time flew by, reminding me of the day the broken school clocks were being fixed and reset and the clock hand went around and around, faster and faster. And I was getting more and more nervous about the party.

I phoned the hospital to speak to Mr. Alexandrov as soon as I got home. But the Information person said he'd already been discharged. I was glad he was better, only I was disappointed too. I'd really wanted to tell him about walking the route and also remind him of his promise to stop by and say hello as soon as he could. Then I'd see for sure if my mother knew him.

Next Mom, Dad, Jillie, Beth, and I started straightening up the kitchen and family room. We always do things at the last minute and say how someday we'll really get organized.

I was complaining about mopping the kitchen floor when

Dad said, "When you're finished mopping the floor, Karen, how about sweeping the cinders around the fireplace?"

"We don't have a fireplace," I said before I caught on to his Cinderella joke. "That was funny, Dad. That was really funny," I said.

As we all raced around getting the house cleaned, my family looked like a scene in a speeded-up silent movie I saw on Channel 13.

Beth was still being nice to me. "Go ahead with Dad and take Jillie shopping for the party stuff. I'll help Mom finish up here."

"Thanks," I said.

It was in the car on the way to the supermarket that I dropped the news of the two extra kids from homeroom.

"Uh, Dad?" I said. "I'm sorry."

"About what?" He asked.

"About what I'm going to tell you—about inviting two more kids to my party without asking permission first. It just happened. They kind of invited themselves."

"Only two more?" Dad said, and to my surprise added, "That's pretty good. Back in my day, in Brooklyn, half the school would have invited themselves by now. You must have handled the situation very well."

I smiled. "You're in such a good mood. Your project must be completed, huh?"

"Just a few loose ends to tighten tomorrow," he said.

Mom was not in as good a mood. She was not pleased to hear about the two extra kids. "Karen," she said when we were home unloading the packages. "No more surprises, okay? Enough is enough."

"I open the door for the kids, right?" Jillie interrupted, repeating her assigned job for the twentieth time.

"Right!" I said.

At six o'clock I picked up the phone and dialed without hesitating a minute. I ordered the party pizza, feeling more friendly toward Alexander Graham Bell. Somehow I felt closely related by now. Alexander Graham Bell seemed to be a part of my daily life. I decided to do my next research paper on him.

We made quick work of an early dinner of chicken pot pie. Then I really got nervous, and as usual I started to scream at the whole family as if it was everyone else's fault. I tore through the house looking for a certain velour top. "Beth, do you have my blue V-neck velour?" I shouted.

"No," she answered, "but I think I know where it is. I'll help you in a second, when I'm off the phone."

"It's impossible to find anything in *this* house!" I yelled. I wished for a moment our house was more organized, like in Allison's house, where shirts and underwear seem to be fed up through the drawer, neatly folded, whenever you want them.

"Try putting something away for a change and you might find it," Mom called. Those were definitely the words of my mom at thirty-eight. I would not ask about secret loves now.

With Jillie's and Beth's help I finally found my blue velour shirt in the dryer, looking like it was permanently pleated, because I'd been too busy to fold it the night before. I set up the ironing board and hoped for the best.

"Iron it inside out," Dad instructed, calling into the laundry room from the kitchen. "And the iron can't be too hot."

"I know what I'm doing!" I yelled.

"You better smile when you talk in that tone," Dad said, his voice firm. I knew I better cool it—my tone, not the iron. Allison's mother irons everything for her and even darns socks. Well, my mother darns socks too, I guess. She looks at the sock with the hole in it, waves it, and says, "Darn socks!"

I pulled out the plug of the iron and admired the good job I'd done. I picked up a pile of clean towels that were on the dryer waiting to be put away and headed for the bathroom. I was getting undressed and ready to take a shower when I heard the doorbell, so I just listened to hear who it was instead of racing to answer the door like Jillie and Beth. It couldn't be the kids already. It was too early for them.

"Ma," I heard Beth call, "there's a man at the door."

"He has a funny green hat on," I heard Jillie say to Beth, and giggle. "He looks like Santa with a new hat. And he's carrying a stick!" They didn't open the door. We're not allowed to open the door for strangers. If only I were dressed. He wasn't a stranger to me. I wanted to speak to Mr. Alexandrov. I also wanted to see my mother's reaction when she saw him. Would she know him?

14

The Party

I wished Beth had stayed at the front door to watch Mom's reaction when she opened it and saw Mr. Alexandrov, but Beth raced off to answer the phone. I also wished that the bathroom, from where I was listening, was even closer than it was to the front door. I wanted to peek out. But at least I could listen hard and still hear Mom and Mr. Alexandrov, although they didn't talk as loudly as Beth and Jillie.

I'm sure I heard Mom open the door and greet him with a smile in her voice. And I'm sure I heard him say, "I promised Karen I'd stop by as soon as I was out of the hospital so she'd know I wasn't hurt."

Then I heard Mom say, "My goodness, I haven't seen you in ages. Come on in. I had no idea all this snowball business was about you. I'm glad you're feeling better."

"I'm perfectly fine. The tests were all negative. I'm as good as new," Mr. Alexandrov said.

"I know Karen will want to see you, but she can't come to the door right now," Mom explained.

Was she glad I couldn't come to the door? And wasn't she afraid Dad would see Mr. Alexandrov? How could she invite Mr. X in there like that? I heard him say that he couldn't stay. He was on his way to do a favor for a friend at the hospital.

"Tell him to stop back later for some pizza when the kids are here. I really want to see him," I called from the bathroom. But she didn't repeat my message. Purposely?

"Just tell Karen I'm feeling fine," Mr. Alexandrov said. Then he told Mom, "It's good to see you again. You look as bright and cheerful as the way you've decorated this room."

I was deciding whether I should quickly throw my clothes back on and race out there instead of showering when I heard the door close. Too late. He was gone. It sure sounded more and more to me like he was Mr. X. I couldn't believe it.

I caught a glimpse of myself in the mirror and decided to wash my hair fast. It must be after seven by now. In less than an hour eight kids would be arriving. But my hair was gross. It looked all frizzy and the ends were split. My hair was not shiny and bouncy the way I wanted it to be with Peter coming here.

Just as I stepped into the shower Jillie screamed, "Allison's on the phone."

"I'll call her back," I yelled over the sound of the water.

Back in my room, I had to keep turning my hair dryer on and off because Allison called again, then Scott called. They both seemed as nervous as I was.

My bedroom soon began to look like a department store bargain basement. I tried a skirt on and took it off. I dumped it on my bed, tried on another skirt, took it off and piled it on top. I decided not to wear the velour after all—I might sweat in it. Then I called Allison to see if she was definitely wearing a skirt. Last minute, we both switched to corduroy straight legs, plaid blouses, and rope belts. "Beth, where is my rope belt?" I yelled.

At seven fifty-eight I was still not dressed. I figured that must be worth points in any Procrastinators' Club. At eight o'clock sharp Scott and Lori arrived. Then, one after another, the rest of the kids turned up and the doorbell kept ringing. Jillie and Beth let the kids in and led them to the basement. Then while Beth stayed with them, Jillie raced to my room to tell me who'd arrived.

"Hurry, Karen, hurry," she said as I struggled with my pants zipper, making sure it was locked shut.

"Tell them I'll be right down," I instructed. Then I figured I better give her a job quickly or she'd sit and tell them how I was busy with my zipper. "You can serve the popcorn while I finish dressing," I said. "Mom already popped it. It's in plastic bags on the kitchen counter."

"Okay," she said and raced off in her usual skid. She didn't even put her shoes on for company.

Jillie takes her work very seriously, I noticed when I joined the group in the basement. All the kids were eating popcorn, even those who didn't want any, because if you didn't take some, she'd kind of push the bowl in your face. I tried to enter the room without tripping down the steps, and I succeeded, but I laughed a new, silly laugh. I don't know where it came from.

Mom and Dad came downstairs to say hello. "Did Beth and Jillie tell you who was here before?" Mom asked.

"Yes," I said, figuring she didn't want to say more with Dad right there. Then I glanced at Dana. She was wearing her hair in a long braid, and her gray corduroy pants were the same as Lori's. I checked to see if she had a cigarette out. She didn't. Not yet, anyway. She just sat on the couch with Allison, Tina, and Lori. The four boys sat on the other couch, opposite them. They sat at the edge, not leaning back. They all seemed to clear their throats a lot.

I introduced Dana, Joey, Tina, and Ron, the four kids my

parents didn't know. I also checked to see that the door to
Dad's lab was closed. It was. I wished Dad had a lock on
the lab door, but he'd never gotten around to getting one. I
didn't want anyone to get near Dad's completed project.
Then, as promised, my parents and Beth started toward
the stairs. "You look super," Dad whispered as he walked
past me.

"Have fun. Yell if you need us," Mom added. Dad put
his hand on Mom's hip as they went upstairs to the kitchen.

"Jillie," Dad called.

"There's still more popcorn," Jillie called back.

"Never mind," Mom called. "Just pop yourself upstairs
and leave Karen and her friends alone."

"Oh, Jillie," Peter said, taking a handful of popcorn, "my
sister Nancy says hi!"

"Give her this piece of popcorn for me," Jillie said,
stuffing a soggy piece she'd been handling to death into
Peter's hand. Then she smiled and raced upstairs. I could
picture her skidding on the floor above in her own sock-
footed way. But she wasn't gone for long. Soon she escaped
and came running downstairs.

She just *had* to sing us the song she learned in kindergarten, she announced. And before Mom could grab her, we
all listened to her sing "B-i-n-g-o, B-i-n-g-o, B-i-n-g-o, and
Bingo was his name!" At least that song wasn't as long as
her usual "Farmer in the Dell." Mom led her upstairs
promising this wouldn't happen again.

At least Beth listened. I'd told her she could come down
for a slice when the pizza came but the rest of the time was
for us older kids only. She'd gone upstairs without a fuss.

The worst part of the party was the beginning. We all
stared at each other. Even Dana was mute, but at least she
didn't light up a cigarette, although I did see a bulge in her

pants pocket about the size of a cigarette pack. Then Ron started tossing an occasional piece of popcorn at Tina, who shrieked and picked the popcorn out of her tightly permed hair. Tina's the kind of kid who shrieks about anything.

Lori was fixing Allison's barrette. I stole another look at the bulge in Dana's pocket. I decided, if she asked for a match, I'd say I couldn't find one. You really can't find anything in our house anyway.

Scott and Allison had brought their favorite albums and I'd let Beth help me choose from the records we share. She loves music and was a big help. I decided to do some of the things from the fifties. We could rate songs by how well you could dance to them, and maybe play Post Office—if I had the nerve to start the game. And do some eighties things, like dancing and Truth or Dare. But I'd forgotten to plan one thing. How to get started doing anything. I put on the Styx album, but no one danced.

That's when I was really glad I'd invited Joey Dillon. He has the amazing ability, like Jell-O, to take the shape of the container it's in. He's just comfortable wherever he is, I guess. He just started the Truth or Dare game by getting up from the couch and taking a comb from his back pocket. He knelt down on the bricklike tile floor and spun the comb around. "The side with the teeth asks Truth or Dare, and the handle side receives," he said.

We all got up and gathered around Joey. We sat on the floor watching the spinning comb. Maybe he's not going to be a tycoon when he grows up, I thought. Maybe he's going to be a game-show host. Finally the comb stopped spinning. Wouldn't you know, the side with the teeth pointed to Dana and the handle side to Peter.

"Truth or Dare?" Dana asked, jumping around in excitement.

"Truth," Peter answered, and took a deep breath.

I was glad Peter said "Truth," because who knows what Dana would think up to dare! She might dare him to smoke or something. Then what would I do? I waited to hear the question.

"I had a dare all ready for you, Peter," Dana moaned. "Now I have to think up a question. Help, someone. I'm not good at questions. Come on, I need a question, somebody."

There were a few questions I wished I had the nerve to call out, but I didn't. Kids started shouting out questions. In Truth or Dare everyone wants to yell out stuff—even if you don't need a question, you get help.

"I've got one," Lori said loudly. "Who do you like? Ask Peter that one, Dana. What girl he likes." Lori said "Ow" and turned to Scott as if he had poked her.

"Who *do* you like?" Dana asked Peter. I waited for Peter to answer.

"Who do I like? What girl?" Peter repeated the questions as if embarrassed and stalling for time.

"Come on, Peter. Answer already," Allison said, being her usual impatient self. She reached for the comb. But Dana held onto it.

"What's the dare you had in mind?" Peter asked Dana.

"I dare you to kiss Karen," she said and smiled.

I almost fainted. I could not figure her out at all.

"I change my mind. I'll take the dare," Peter said, "but I'll do it later."

"Chicken," Joey said and clucked, but Peter didn't seem embarrassed. He just didn't say a word more, and the kids stopped teasing.

I felt like my heart had stopped beating and I'd surely die in a minute or so.

"Okay," Dana said and spun the comb.

Jeff, who is very team-spirited at basketball games said, "Come on, comb!" Whatever that meant.

All I heard after that was my own heartbeat. I guess I'd even postponed dying. Was Peter going to kiss me right here in front of everybody? That's when I'd die. I didn't care so much about being embarrassed about little things anymore, but I wasn't immune to embarrassment. There was no Salk vaccine for it, like for polio.

The comb handle pointed at Lori. Scott said, "Truth or Dare?"

"Truth," Lori said.

"Okay," Scott said. "Who would you like to sit next to while going through the spook house at Great Adventure?"

"Joey Dillion," Lori answered, to Scott's surprise.

"Not me?" Scott said.

Lori laughed and explained. "Joey Dillon could spook the spooks." And we all laughed.

Then Lori dared Joey Dillon to put his arm around Dana for three minutes. He did it—no trouble at all. Lori walked over and sat down next to Scott. He smiled at her.

I thought the game was over, but then Dana gave me one last dare, and it was a beauty. "Ooh, Karen," she said. "I dare you to show us that your dad really makes bionic hands like the kids say. What is he, Frankenstein?" she said laughing.

"Ooh yeah. Let's see it," Jeff chimed in. "I love electronics."

"Karen's dad works right here in the basement—back there in his lab," Scott said, pointing to the door. "Sometimes he lets me help him," he added proudly.

I know Scott loves that. His own father doesn't have much time for him. I remember once, when Scott was little, he told his dad that when he grew up he'd like to be a patient. Scott loves to talk about my dad's work. But tonight I wished he'd kept his mouth shut.

The kids headed for the door to the lab. Oh no! I thought. One false move and Dad's project could fall and get broken. But I wanted to be one of the group. It would be fun to show them the bionic hand so they'd know it was true. I was very proud of my dad's work. Even Peter was saying "Neato."

"We'll be real careful," Scott said. "No one will touch a thing. We'll just peek, okay?"

But I had this feeling again. Deep inside me. The same feeling I had when I heard Mr. Alexandrov had been hurt and it might have been my snowball that hurt him. I'd made my own decision. I wouldn't just listen to what the other kids were saying. And whatever happened, I was ready for it. Dana already had her hand on the doorknob and was turning it.

No. I was not going to take a chance with four years of Dad's work just so I wouldn't be embarrassed. I pushed her hand off the doorknob and blocked the doorway with my body. "Sorry, guys," I said firmly. "The lab is off limits. I promised." I wished my mom would do something like bring the pizza, but no such luck. She probably hadn't even gone out for it yet.

"Aw, come on, Karen," Dana pleaded. "Let me see the bionic hand."

I just changed the subject, turned on the record player, and got everyone interested in rating songs like in the fifties. But after two songs that was boring. Then Dana reached into her back pocket, and I thought for sure she was going to take out a pack of cigarettes, light up, smoke, and then charge into the lab. But when she pulled out the box that bulged in her pocket, it was a pack of cards.

"Dana's terrific at card tricks," Peter announced. "Show them," he encouraged her.

"Yeah," I added, and the party went on, with the bionic hand remaining untouched. I was relieved about that, but I also wondered how Peter knew so much about Dana.

Dana was happy as could be. She really had all our attention when she did the tricks, and she even taught us this trick where you put all the cards in order before anyone sees them.

"You arrange them ace, two, three, up to king," she said. "You do the same for hearts, spades, clubs, and diamonds. Then you ask a kid to pick a card. Then you take the rest of the cards in your hand and look at them," Dana went on. "You guess the missing card—and you look brilliant!"

"How do you know which one it is?" Jeff asked.

"You know which one it is because the cards are all in order, so you can tell what's missing—the missing number in the suit."

"Excellent." Scott said.

I tried the trick out on Peter. First he got mixed up with the numbers, but I showed him again. The trick really works.

At nine o'clock, probably because we were making a lot of noise and laughing at anything anyone said, Mom and Beth announced that they were going out to pick up the pizza. So they weren't home when the doorbell rang. Dad and Jillie brought Mr. Alexandrov down to see me. I wondered if Mom had seen Mr. Alexandrov returning and had arranged to be out.

"Karen," Mr. Alexandrov said, greeting me. He pulled off his green woolen hat, and to my surprise, he was bald on top. "I'm all better," he added. "And I've already heard from a few sources that you did a good job on the morning walk."

"Great," I said.

"I just wanted you to see for yourself how good I look so you wouldn't be worried. A promise is a promise. In the hospital I promised you that the very next time I passed your house, I'd stop in and say hello to you. As you can see, I'm a man who keeps his word. I didn't see you when I stopped by earlier, but I heard you call and invite me back later. So here I am."

"But aren't you weak from being hurt?" I asked.

"Just a little tired now and then. They put you in bed, you get tired. I kept telling the doctors there was nothing wrong with me, but all they want to do is tests, tests, tests. So what did their tests show? That there's nothing wrong with me. That's what!"

"Do you walk at night too?" I asked.

"No. At night I drive," he said.

I'd never thought of Mr. Alexandrov driving. It seemed funny. I wanted to be polite, but I also wanted to get on with my party. This wasn't exactly a good time for a visit, when my mother wasn't even home to react. What was taking her so long anyway?

"My mom will be right back. She went to pick up pizza for my party."

Then I was in for another surprise when I introduced the other kids.

"Peter and Dana?" Mr. Alexandrov asked. "Peter Raskin and Dana Winters, by any chance?"

"Yes," I said.

"How nice to meet you," Mr. Alexandrov said to them. "Call me Charlie, and thank you for the plant and the get-well note you sent to the hospital."

"It was nothing," Dana said, and Peter kind of blushed and mumbled, "Glad you liked it. We were real sorry you got hurt."

I liked Peter even more now. And I couldn't help thinking twice about Dana.

"Go on with your party, my friends," Mr. Alexandrov said. "I'll see you around. And no more snowballs. A wave 'hello' will do." He started back up the stairs. "And, Karen," he called down, "I just drove back from the hospital. Morris is doing fine. Still yelling 'I'm dying,' but his gall bladder is out and he's very much alive. Remember, we have a date to play gin."

"I remember," I said, and waved as Mr. Alexandrov left. I explained to the others about Morris. "I didn't know you knew Mr. Alexandrov," I said to Dana and Peter.

"We didn't know him," Peter said. "Sending the plant was just an idea that popped into my head. My folks always say I'm impulsive. Dana helped me write the note. I guess it made *us* feel better."

The rest of the kids started talking about the day the ambulance came to school and about the snowballs and the postponed dance. I wished Mom and Beth would hurry, because I didn't know what to do next at this party of mine. But they hadn't come back. Had they met Mr. Alexandrov outside and stopped to talk? Finally Mom and Beth returned with the pizza. Mom put the boxes out on a table and Beth gave us paper plates and napkins.

"Sorry it took so long," Mom said. "The pies weren't ready. The owner of the pizza place thought your phone order for three pies on a Thursday night was a crank call. So we had to wait while he got the pizza ready for us. Dig in. Self-service." she added, taking three slices back upstairs for Dad, Jillie, and herself.

Beth really enjoyed eating her pizza with us. She even was fun to be with, acting just like any other kid. I couldn't pick the cheese off my slice like I usually do. It wouldn't look cool in front of Peter. I found out I've grown up to like the cheese on pizza too. But I still like the crust best. Jillie calls it "pizza bones," because people leave the crust on their plates. I also tried to eat the pizza so that oil wouldn't drip down my arm. It was pretty quiet while we all ate.

I hoped I didn't have any specks of oregano caught between my braces, because I was expecting a kiss in the near future. Peter still had that dare to take care of. Beth went upstairs just in time. All my family were two rooms away in the den watching TV, so the kitchen was good and private. I knew the moment my kiss was coming, when we played Post Office and Peter called my name, and I went upstairs into the kitchen with him. Joey closed the door behind us. I was glad he also turned out the lights. I waited for Peter to kiss me.

"I'm glad we're alone," Peter said, and I could feel my heart beat.

I tried to remember how people kiss on TV and in the movies. But Peter wasn't kissing. He was talking.

"I want to explain to you about Dana," he said, just standing next to me, leaning against the sink, not me. "I should have told you all this on the phone yesterday, but like with sending the plant, things just pop into my mind. I kind of blurt things out without thinking. I always have, the same way I've always reversed numbers. Dana's like that too, only her folks and friends don't help her like mine do."

"What do you mean?" I asked, simply because they were the only words that I could think of.

"I'm not sure how to tell you this." Peter chewed on his

bottom lip, then went on. "Dana and I went to first, second, and third grade together in this special school for learning disabilities. I've been in regular school four years now, but this is Dana's first year back. She's not handling it. She acts up or fools around so people won't think she's dumb."

All I could say was, "What do you mean?" and stare at the way Peter's shirt was partly untucked on the side, as usual.

"Dana knows she didn't come to your party as my date or anything. I just wanted her to feel she belongs and doesn't have to get in trouble to get attention. I remember how it feels," Peter added, and he reached for my hand. "When I started special school, Dana showed me around and helped me," Peter said, before we were interrupted by Joey Dillon, who whistled a flirting kind of wolf whistle and called, "What's going on up there?"

And Scott called, "You okay, Karen?"

"Yeah," I called back, not very loudly. I was okay. It felt good to share something important, not just a joke, like our telephone code names, Andrew and Rebecca. Besides, it was easy to be understanding and help Dana when Peter got impulsive again and was kissing *me!* I kind of held my breath and kissed him back. I think our kiss tasted like pizza—delicious.

In general, I'd stopped getting so embarrassed, but I knew I was blushing when we went back downstairs. Especially when Joey said, "Guess Peter's no chicken after all." And Tina shrieked.

Before the party was over, Tina and Ron, the kids from homeroom who had invited themselves to my party, were the only ones with nerve enough to dance in this group, which was too small to get lost in. But when no one else joined them, they stopped. Jeff just had to watch the ten o'clock TV news sportscast and he turned on the old set we have in the basement. Allison gave him one of her murderous looks, then kind of shrugged her shoulders and sat down next to him to ask dumb questions. Scott and Lori were sitting on the couch holding hands, and Peter whispered to me, "I always thought you liked Scott, not me."

"We're just really good friends, Scott and me. Like you and Dana."

Then like clockwork, one hour later, we were all struck with pizza thirst, the kind of thirst that even soda doesn't quench. We had more fun with group trips to the kitchen than we'd had with our planned games. We'd already finished the soda, so we tried to drink down glasses of water in one breath. Joey Dillon had us doubled up laughing when he demonstrated drinking from the far side of the cup and water dribbled down his shirt. Pizza thirst is never quenched with one glass of water. I hoped my stomach wouldn't gurgle, it might be embarrassing, I thought. I heard a gurgle and I automatically rubbed my stomach. Then I realized Lori and Tina were rubbing theirs too. We each thought it was our own stomach. I laughed and relaxed.

The rest of the evening seemed to go by as fast as a falling star. All the kids left a little after eleven-thirty, picked up by parent car-pool drivers. On the way out Joey Dillon held the door open for Dana. Peter told them to go on ahead to the car, that he'd be right there.

He would have been last to leave—the way I'd hoped—but Dana forgot her comb and had to come back for it. She got it and I opened the door quickly before she walked through it on her way out again. She moves so fast. She practically walked backward down the path to where her father waited, honking the car horn impatiently. She kept waving to me calling, "See you in school. Nice party. I'm glad Peter likes you."

I felt glad that Dana looked so happy. I also felt freezing cold and closed the door. I just stood there for a moment with my nose pressed flat against one of the small windows next to the front door. I watched the car Peter, Dana and Joey were in until it was out of sight. And then like a rewound movie, I played back the party in my mind and held on the screen the moments of the kiss scene.

15

The Diary

Mom and Dad were in the kitchen drinking glass after glass
of water when I walked in and collapsed onto a chair. They
said they'd just checked the bedroom, and Jillie and Beth
were sound asleep. They'd been allowed to stay up until
ten-thirty as planned. Then I remembered the condition of
the basement and I popped up.

Mom and Dad went with me to the basement and helped
collect the dirty soda cups. I hadn't asked them to—in fact,
I'd said, "I'll do it." I was glad there were no cigarette ashes
to empty or explain. I picked up the pretzel and popcorn
droppings and dumped them into the garbage. Then we
went upstairs and sat down at the kitchen table. I waited
for the question they usually ask, betting on who would ask
it first, Mom or Dad. I thought it would be Dad.

"Well?" Mom began.

And Dad finished, "How was it?"

"Good," I said. "The party was real good," I added, and
we hugged. I didn't tell Mom and Dad about the close call
with the bionic hand—or about the kiss and conversation.
That was between Peter and me. Some things are just
private. I wondered if Mom's missing diary pages and my

thoughts about Mr. X and Mr. Alexandrov should remain private too. But I still wanted to ask about it all. I didn't have to know everything, but a little more would sure help. I did hint about kissing. "They don't call that game Post Office anymore," I laughed. "Joey Dillon called it Seven Minutes in Heaven."

"Seven minutes?" Dad said. "Inflation's hit everything!" He laughed.

Then he got a serious look, kind of happy and sad at the same time, when I said dreamily, "Peter likes me. He really does."

"I'm glad you're happy," Dad said, and he put one arm around my mom and one arm around me and hugged us both. Sometimes my dad speaks sentences with a hug and punctuates with a kiss on my forehead. That's what he did. Then we headed for our rooms. "It's not easy for fathers to let daughters go, you know," he called. "But it is interesting—definitely interesting."

I couldn't fall asleep. So instead of telling my secrets to my parakeet, Bruno, or reading Mom's diary, or writing a memo, I started a diary of my own.

February, 1980
Dear Diary, I did it? I decided to have a party, and it was good. And Peter kissed me and that was good too . . .

I wrote five pages. As I folded down a corner on the last page I heard Mom settling down to write in the kitchen, making herself some coffee. It was only 2 A.M., early according to Mom Standard Time, I thought, as I glanced at my alarm clock. I put on my robe and fuzzy slippers, tucked my diary under my arm, and headed for the kitchen.

I went in quietly so I wouldn't disturb Mom if she was in the middle of a thought. She has a writing rule about that, the only exception being cuts and bruises. I listened to the sound of her pencil racing on the yellow pad and sniffed the smell of fresh coffee. Soon she looked up. The house was so quiet except for the faucet dripping an occasional drop.

"Here," I said, and handed her my own diary. "You can read the page I folded down." Somehow I knew she'd only read the page I said she could read, and not the other pages about Peter and the kiss. I liked trusting her. I sat down at the table on the chair next to her.

Mom read the page I wanted her to see, about how I was glad she'd given me her diary so I could see she was once scared and embarrassed too. So I could read about her being happy or sad, even silly. And especially so I could find out she was in love now and then, like me.

Mom hugged me. She whispered that she had two more diaries about the next two years, but she was saving them for Beth and Jillie.

"I'm glad," I said and meant it. I like things to be fair. It's one of my favorite words.

I knew we were doing it again like the night when she gave me her diary, leaving a wet tear spot on each other's shoulder. And I figured, maybe there'd be times when I'd cry angry tears, but I knew for sure that these moments together at 2 A.M. were special.

"My baby's growing up," Mom said.

"I'll always be your baby?" I asked.

"Kind of," Mom said, "but I like the way you're growing up, because now you're my friend too." We both were quiet a minute, then Mom said, "Hey, I'm driving into the city on Sunday, want to come, and we'll get twofer tickets for a Broadway matinee?"

"Yeah," I said, "I'd love to." I reached over and hugged her again and she hugged me back.

"Karen, fight me if I hold onto you too tightly," she whispered and stroked my hair.

"I will," I said. "In fact, on the next snowy day I'll wear only one boot to school," I said, but I was half serious too, "to show you I'll listen to some things but I need one foot free. I like that line," I added. "I think I'll write it in my diary."

Mom smiled, and I knew that now, when we were feeling close, was the right time to ask. "Speaking of diaries," I said, like Johnny Carson easing into a commercial, "I've got a couple of questions about yours."

"I was wondering when you were going to ask about those missing pages. You waited longer than I ever would," Mom said.

I took a deep breath and dove right in. "And I also want to know about Mr. X. Will you tell me who he is?" My hands started to get a cold feeling.

"I'll do better than just tell you," she said. "I'll show him to you."

My heart started to pound. Maybe it really was Mr. Alexandrov, and next time he walked by Mom would show him to me.

"Do you still have the ripped-out diary pages?" I asked.

"Come with me," Mom said and smiled, "and we'll straighten this all out."

I figured she was leading me to her bedroom to get the diary pages, so I was really surprised when we opened the door and she turned on the lamp next to the bed. Dad gave a loud snore, and I thought for sure he'd wake up, and then what? Mom didn't move, though. She just looked at Dad and said to me, "So now you know."

"I do?" I asked feeling confused.

Dad snored and pulled the covers over his head.

"You're looking at him, Karen," Mom said, and pointed to the mountain of moving blanket in the bed. "That's my Mr. X," she said, pointing to my dad. "I married him. And he snores," she added, "but I love him anyway."

"I do not snore," Dad grumbled sleepily, rolled over, fell back to sleep, and snored. Mom and I laughed.

"Dad is Mr. X?" I couldn't believe it. "But what about Mr. Alexandrov who walks by our house every day? I heard him come to the door this evening, and you knew him. I could tell."

"Of course I know him," Mom said. "Your dad knows him too."

"He does?" I asked.

And Mom explained. "We've even mentioned him to you years ago when he lived in town. You probably never paid it much attention. It's nice that he's come back. We bought this house from him. You were just a baby then. He even built it—and a few other houses in this neighborhood. What a nice old man he is."

That reminded me. "But I thought Mr. X was an older man. That's what your diary said. Dad's not that much older than you."

"It's a funny thing about age," Mom said, stroking my hair again. "Sure, Dad's only five years older than I am, but when I was your age and he was in high school, that was a big difference. To Grandma and Grandpa he was definitely an older man. But all of a sudden, when I was a junior in high school and he was in college, it didn't seem like such an age difference anymore."

"You know what I thought?" I whispered and giggled. "I thought Mr. X was Mr. Alexandrov. His name could even fit it. Al-X-an-drov, Mr. X."

"Yes, Karen, you definitely have got the best imagination in the house." Mom laughed. "Now, do you want to see one of the ripped-out pages? I knew I had them someplace. I've been searching for them. I figured you were going to ask about those pages soon. It's a good thing I'm a saver. Although I couldn't find all the ripped-out pages, I finally found at least one of them, mixed in with some love letters your dad wrote me from college. I'd saved them in a box up in my closet."

"Love letters?" I asked with interest.

"Those are between your dad and me," Mom said. "Not everything is for sharing." Then she kissed me good night. We got up from the bed, where we'd been sitting. Dad rolled over again. Mom led me to her closet and put the page into my hands: May 9, 1955! "Happy dreams," she said, and I went to my room.

I didn't even take off my robe. I just turned on my lamp, curled up on my bed, and read:

May 9, 1955
Hurray! Mr. X noticed me again, and even better than that, he likes me. We walked to Brooklyn College together and sat on the benches by the reflecting pond and talked and talked. He held my hand. Was that a date? I'm so glad I was sent to the avenue for milk— only I forgot to buy it, and we had to stop at Waldbaum's on the way back.

I'm in love. I know this is crazy, but I know I'm in love. And what's even crazier is Mr. X wants me to go out with him. And what's even crazier is he said he's noticed me for a while and he thinks even though it sounds strange now, that some day when we both finish college, he'd like to marry me. Isn't that crazy?

If Judy ever gets hold of this she'll tell Mom and Dad, and how will I explain that I was asked to get married? So I'm not taking any chances. I'm ripping out this page and hiding it. I just had to write this down. I'm writing very small so I can fit it all in, because when I marry Mr. X and if we have kids, I might want to tell them about this day.

I went home and played the record "They Tried to Tell Us We're Too Young." I played it over and over again.

I put May 9, 1955, under my pillow and fell asleep, still wearing my robe, and already dreaming. I think I smiled all night.

The next morning I looked out my window, and at eight o'clock—right on schedule—there he was, Mr. Alexandrov looking at my window from the street. I knocked on the window and waved. He waited for me. I quickly dressed in the first sweater and jeans I grabbed, threw on my coat and sneakers, and raced out to walk with him. I was glad he was just Mr. Alexandrov, my friend, and not my mom's Mr. X.

I walk Mr. Alexandrov's morning route with him every day now. Sometimes Beth or Jillie comes too. And every day he says the same thing: "I built all these houses. I sanded and varnished every handrail. When you work hard, Karen, and make something, it brings you joy in your old age. And your house, Karen, with you and your family living there, and you walking with me, makes this old man very happy."

MEMO: To myself.
I think I love Mr. Alexandrov. It's just a friendship
love, and that's special. He's taught me the names of
the birds around here and their calls, and we walk
and bird-watch and feed the birds together. I guess
you might say our friendship is for the birds—ha-ha.

Of course I still love Peter. And we're going to the
Madison School's Procrastinators' Sadie Hawkins Day
Dance this weekend. Some days Peter, Dana, Allison, and
Scott walk with Mr. Alexandrov and me. And on Friday
afternoons we all go visit Morris in the nursing home,
where he's getting better after some complications from his
gall bladder operation. Dana does card tricks and then we
all play gin rummy. Now Morris doesn't say "I'm dying."
He just moans, "Another ace? You're killing me."

I still read Mom's diary. Especially if we've had a fight. I
wonder if she'll ever show me those love letters? And will I
someday have love letters of my own? I wonder if I'll want
to get married someday after I become a scientist? And if
I'll ever have kids to show my diaries and memos to?

I don't worry so much anymore. I don't have time to.
But I do wonder a lot!

BOOKS FOR TODAY'S TEENAGERS

☐ 0-425-09575-4	**THE GREEN OF ME** Patricia Lee Gauch	$2.50
☐ 0-425-10341-2	**THE GIRL WHO WANTED TO RUN THE BOSTON MARATHON** Robert McKay	$2.50
☐ 0-425-09596-7	**PLEASE SEND JUNK FOOD** Susan Schneider	$2.50
☐ 0-425-09709-9	**THE LEFTOVER KID** Carole Snyder	$2.50
☐ 0-425-08448-5	**WANTED: DATE FOR SATURDAY NIGHT** Janet Quin-Harkin	$2.50
☐ 0-425-08867-7	**THE PLOT AGAINST THE POM-POM QUEEN** Ellen Leroe	$2.50
☐ 0-425-08449-3	**ARE WE THERE YET?** Wendy Andrews	$2.50
☐ 0-425-08881-2	**BREAKING UP IS HARD TO DO** Meg F. Schneider	$2.50
☐ 0-425-08425-6	**MY OWN WORST ENEMY** Margot B. McDonnell	$2.50
☐ 0-425-08885-5	**WART, SON OF TOAD** Alden R. Carter	$2.50
☐ 0-425-11277-2	**SKI BUM** Helane Zeiger (On sale December '88)	$2.50

From Award-winning Storyteller

IRENE HUNT

_____ **ACROSS FIVE APRILS**   0-425-10241-6/$2.75
The unforgettable story of a young boy's coming of age
during the turbulent Civil War.
A Newbery Honor Medal Book!

_____ **THE LOTTERY ROSE**   0-425-10153-3/$2.75
The poignant novel of a young boy, abused by his mother
and her boyfriend, who finds solace in the beauty of
his own private world.

_____ **NO PROMISES IN THE WIND**   0-425-09969-5/$2.75
The intriguing story of a fifteen-year-old boy who
discovers the pains and joys of growing up during the
Depression years.

_____ **UP A ROAD SLOWLY**   0-425-10003-0/$2.75
The beautiful and memorable story of a pretty, young
girl's climb from seven to seventeen.
A Newbery Award Winning Novel!

HEATHCLIFF

by
George
Gately

AMERICA'S FUNNIEST FELINE!